Creativ
Embr

Divine Messengers by Linda Miller 2003 48 x 30 cm (19 x 12 in.)

Creative Machine Embroidery

Linda Miller

A&C Black•London

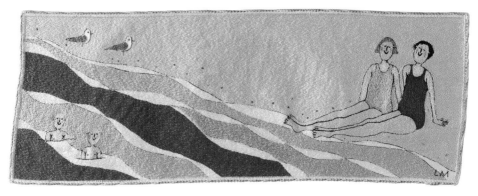

Splashing *by Linda Miller 2008 16 x 42 cm (6¼ x 16½ in.)*

First published in Great Britain in 2010
A&C Black Publishers Limited
36 Soho Square
London W1D 3QY
www.acblack.com

ISBN: 978-14081-0398-2

Typeset in 9 on 14pt Century Gothic

Photography: front and back covers
Michael Jennings
All other photography: Cesca Sims

Book design by Norma Martin
Cover design by James Watson
Commissioning editor: Susan James
Copyediting: Barbara Cheney

Frontispiece by Linda Miller

Printed and bound in Singapore

A&C Black uses paper produced with
elemental chlorine-free pulp, harvested
from managed sustainable forests.

Publisher's note: Every effort has been
made to ensure that the information in
this book is accurate. Due to differing
conditions, tools, materials and individual
skills, the publisher cannot be held
responsible for any injuries, losses and
other damages resulting from the use of
information in this book. You should always
take all safety precautions necessary and
follow manufacturers' health and safety
advice carefully and accurately.

Contents

Acknowledgements

With thanks to:

- Susan James at A&C Black Publishers Ltd for approaching and inspiring me to write this book.

- Sophie Page at A&C Black Publishers Ltd for her encouragement.

- Michael Jennings for motivation, love, support, and the hot drinks.

- Cesca Sims for her photography, styling, encouragement and appreciation of my cats.

- Linda Trueman who first showed me how to machine embroider and how to edge pieces, plus all the technical help, encouragement and praise she gave me throughout the beginning of my machine embroidery journey.

- Whaleys (Bradford) for the calico.

- Front cover: Machine Embroidery by Linda Miller
  Curlews & Shells 2004 39 x 30 cm (15½ x 12 in.) Photo by Michael Jennings
  Back cover: Machine Embroidery by Linda Miller *Blowy Leaves* 2005
  19 x 14 cm (7½ x 5½ in.) Photo by Michael Jennings

- Photographs/photo images by Cesca Sims.

Beach Hut Lunch *by Linda Miller 2009 10 x 10 cm (4 x 4 in.)*

Winter Yarn *by Linda Miller 2008 10 x 13 cm (4 x 5¼ in.)*

Introduction

Machine embroidery is a wonderfully satisfying creative medium and working with your sewing machine to create beautiful embroidery pieces can be very rewarding. The simple pleasure of decorative sewing is an age old tradition which is still embraced today, and although the basics of using a sewing machine have not changed much since its invention, the technology has. Whether you are using a simple domestic electric sewing machine or a computerised one, both allow a wonderful freedom to experiment. The huge range of threads and fabrics on the market today give us even more opportunity to venture with different effects and styles to create an exciting pallet to work with. However, it is down to us to make the best of our tools and to maximise them to their full potential. There is such a diverse range of what can be created, decorated and achieved with machine embroidery. It is ceaseless and continues to inspire and delight not only the maker but the devotee as well.

The aim of this book is to explain simply how you can design and make embroidery pieces using a sewing machine. Working with your sewing machine and your chosen array of threads, you will be guided through all aspects of creating a design, placing imagery, and finishing and presenting your pieces effectively. This will enable you to gain a greater understanding of the machine embroidery process and what can be achieved with this textile medium.

The exciting and easy to understand step-by-step projects (see pages 21 and 77-120) will help you to find your own creative style and confidence. Whether you are a novice or a more experienced stitcher, you will be encouraged and inspired to use your own ideas and materials. Working at your own speed and with your own unique style, you can explore the numerous techniques and textures created by threads and stitch, and in the process discover the delight of sewing and working with colour.

1 Tools

In all of the projects to make in Chapter 10, the following basic tools are required. An additional list of materials is given at the beginning of each project.

YOU WILL NEED

Basic tools

- An electric sewing machine, in good working order which can lower its feed dog (teeth situated in the base plate) or has a plate that can fit over the feed dog and that can do a zigzag stitch as well as a straight stitch
- The sewing machine manual and sewing machine tool kit
- A machine embroidery or darning foot that is compatible with your sewing machine
- Size 12/80 sewing machine needles
- Hand sewing needles
- Plenty of bobbin spools: make sure they are compatible with your sewing machine; different machines have different sized bobbins
- A wooden 25.5 cm (10 in.) embroidery hoop with a screw fitting that can be tightened using a screwdriver
- A standard screwdriver that will fit the screw on the embroidery hoop
- Dressmaking scissors
- Embroidery scissors with sharp points
- Heavyweight calico
- Machine embroidery threads and/or any machine threads you have in 30 and 40 weights, in various colours
- Hand embroidery threads in various colours
- Stabilising fabric
- Coloured pencils
- An HB pencil

Equipment for machine embroidery

- Drawing paper
- Masking tape
- Note pad and pen
- A fabric drawing pen
- A steam iron and an ironing board

This is a standard list of tools and items that you need to begin freestyle machine embroidery. Of course as you develop your own style, skill and knowledge of how the process works, you will no doubt want to explore and widen your range of materials and accessories.

Health and safety precautions

- Make sure your sewing machine is fused, earthed and in good working order.
- If you have long hair keep it tied back to prevent it getting tangled in the machine.
- It does not matter whether you are new to working with a sewing machine or whether you have spent many competent years sewing, whenever your fingers are near to the needle of the machine make sure that your foot is not on the pedal. It only takes one slight movement of your foot to activate the machine and cause the needle to move. You want the needle to go into fabric and not your fingers.
- When operating your sewing machine always make sure that you are sitting comfortably and that your chair and table are correctly adjusted for your height and stature. This helps to prevent back and neck ache. It is wise also to get up and walk about after 20 minutes or so of intensive sewing as this action (apart from preventing aches) can be beneficial to your work. When you return to it you may find that you see what you are making with 'fresh eyes'.
- Good lighting is very important when working on any art or craft project and working at a sewing machine is no exception. If your eyes have to work harder than necessary due to poor lighting conditions they will tire quickly and your machine embroideries will suffer wobbly lines. Clear, natural daylight is ideal but rarely achievable, and using a daylight simulation bulb is a good alternative.
- Give yourself plenty of room to work in. A cluttered space is indicative of a cluttered mind so if you have any clutter, clear it away and free up your mind.

2 Sewing Machines

Shoreline Birds by
Linda Miller 2008
9 x 18 cm
(3½ x 7 in.)

The most important piece of equipment that you need for freestyle machine embroidery is an electric sewing machine. If you are considering buying a new or reconditioned one there are many different makes and models on the market and choosing the best one for your needs can be a daunting task. If you've never owned a sewing machine, talk to friends and family members who have one and ask to try it out; no doubt they will be very enthusiastic to tell you its good and, if any, bad points. When choosing a machine to buy go to a recognised retailer and ask for a demonstration.

Take your time in choosing a machine to buy as you will have it for many years. Cost will no doubt be a big contributing factor to your choice, so consider what other types of sewing and craft projects you may use your machine for. A general rule is to opt for a good, standard electric machine which can lower its feed dog, has the option of stitching backwards, can sew buttonholes as well as zigzag stitches and a few other fancy stitches besides. Most importantly, make sure it is straightforward to use and easily understood.

For machine embroidery, a sewing machine must either be able to lower its feed dog, or have a plate that can be fitted over the feed dog. The feed dog is situated in the base plate where the needle goes in and out and can be lowered and raised by a switch, or have a plate fitted over it (refer to the sewing machine manual). When using your machine for sewing such as dressmaking and curtain making, the regularity of stitching is controlled by the raised feed dog, which makes an even stitch by 'pulling' the fabric through the machine. When using the machine for freestyle machine embroidery the feed dog needs to be lowered, as it is you and not the feed dog that determines where the stitch line goes.

Your sewing machine needs to have an embroidery foot. Every sewing machine manufacturer has different types of feet and names for machine embroidery. Some refer to it as darning, for instance, so again refer to your manual to make sure that the embroidery foot is compatible with your sewing machine.

Sewing machine tension

The sewing machine tension which is used in freestyle machine embroidery is normally the same as that used for dressmaking and curtain making. However, altering the tension can create different effects within the embroidery. How to create these effects is explained in 'Threads, textures and colour' on page 38.

Sewing machine needles

Different types of fabrics and threads require different thickness and types of sewing machine needles.

The needle number denotes the size and thickness: the higher the number, the thicker the needle. There are usually two needle sizes written on needle packets: Imperial (USA) and metric (Europe). The Imperial numbers are the smaller numbers and the European numbers are the higher numbers, e.g. 9/65, 11/75, 12/80, 14/90, 16/100, 18/110.

 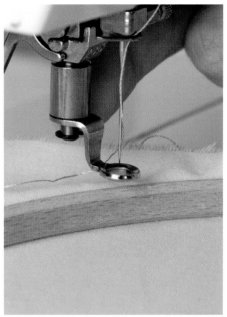

Fitting the embroidery hoop under the needle

Lift the foot with your index finger over the embroidery hoop

You need to choose the correct machine needle for the fabric you are working with. For example, using a large needle on a fine fabric will cause large holes in the stitch line, and using a thin needle on thick fabric will cause the needle to bend or break. You may also find that the stitch line is not complete and will have stitches missing.

In general, a size 12/80 needle is adequate for machine embroidering onto most fabrics. However, for fine fabrics a thinner needle is required, such as a size 9/65 or 11/75, and when using metallic threads, a ball point machine needle or a 'Metallica' needle is recommended.

Use good quality machine needles – the needle is one of the cheapest components of a sewing machine. Change the needle regularly as machine embroidery is comprised of many stitches that can cause the needle to blunt quicker than when using your sewing machine for other craft projects.

Sumptuous threads

Embroidery hoops

For easy freestyle machine embroidering the base fabric needs to be kept taut in an embroidery hoop, allowing the needle to bounce evenly off it and the embroidery that is being created. If the base fabric is too loose it creates a difficult surface to work on.

The best type to use is a simple circular wooden embroidery hoop with a screw on the outer hoop and a plain circular wooden hoop in the middle. The screw is tightened to create the required tension for the fabric being embroidered onto. The hoop can be tightened easily and is narrow enough to be fitted under most machine embroidery feet. If you find it difficult to fit the hoop under the embroidery foot and the foot has a spring incorporated in it, simply place your index finger under the bottom of the foot and lift it. The spring in the foot should allow you to do this. Slide the hoop underneath the machine foot, making sure that the needle is high and out of the way to avoid hitting and possibly breaking the needle, then release your finger from the foot and the spring will automatically revert to the down position. Do not be tempted to use the plastic hoops that have an inside spring. They are perfect for hand embroidery, but for machine embroidery they do not hold the fabric firmly enough.

Crease lines left by the wooden hoop on the embroidery can easily be removed by steam ironing them once the machine embroidery has been completed. Hold the steam iron about 1 cm (¼ in.) away from the front of the embroidery piece and let the steam penetrate it. Then turn the piece over and iron the back of it to get rid of the crease lines. You may need to repeat this process a few times if the crease lines are very deep. Do this process before you have embellished the embroidery with any beads, buttons and trinkets, and make sure that the threads you have used will not melt.

Threads

There is a fantastic array of machine embroidery threads available in sumptuous, sparkling colours, weights and textures, both in man-made and natural fibres. They are readily found in shops, at textile fairs, and on the internet. Tempting though it might be to buy and use cheaper threads when starting out, you will find that they break and shred so easily that you may abandon using them due to lack of progress. So always choose good quality machine embroidery threads.

Of course it can be difficult to know which threads are easy to use and which ones can be problematic, so it is wise to stick to the names and manufacturers that you know before trying others. Choose a general pallet of colours, weights and textures which you can easily add to as you progress. Ask for them as presents – they last much longer than any box of chocolates! Before long you will have a fabulous collection of the most beautiful threads you could ever imagine, to inspire you time and time again. Remember that you can also use standard machine threads such as those used for dressmaking; these have a matt look to them and work very well. Interesting mixes can be achieved when used in conjunction with the machine embroidery threads, which tend to be shiny in appearance.

Hand embroidery threads

Each hand embroidery thread is made up of six strands of cotton and, as the name suggests, they are used primarily for hand embroidery as they are too thick to be used on a sewing machine. However, once the piece has been machine embroidered, hand embroidery threads can be sewn on by hand for extra decoration and embellishment. In 'Projects to make' (page 75), hand embroidery threads are used for edging and the technique is explained in 'Making a sample heart' on page 21.

Getting to know your sewing machine

If your sewing machine is new to you, it is best to first thoroughly read the manual. Sit in front of your machine so you can see what's what, and even if you've had your machine for years it does no harm to refresh your knowledge with the manual.

Try out a few lines of stitches on a waste piece of fabric. If your machine has a selection of fancy and decorative stitches, sample these too as they can be a useful addition to have. Generally play around with the machine to familiarise yourself with it and listen to the sound it makes. If it sounds unhappy or is struggling, stop sewing and sort it out. It can be extremely frustrating if you are halfway through a project and with time against you, but in the long run stopping and sorting out any machine difficulties saves time. If you carry on working with an unhappy machine the chances are you will be disappointed with the end result and feel frustrated with both yourself and your machine. Don't be afraid of it as it is a wonderful tool, and if treated with respect and a certain amount of kindness you will have a happy and creative partnership.

The following is a checklist for dealing with general sewing problems:

- Double check that the sewing machine is threaded correctly; it doesn't take a moment to unthread and thread it again.
- Make sure the bobbin case and bobbin spool are the correct ones for your sewing machine. Not all cases and spools are the same size and therefore not necessarily suited to your machine.
- Check that the bobbin is wound correctly; it should be neither too tight nor too loose.
- Make sure that your bobbin is sitting in the bobbin case the right way round, or if your machine does not have a bobbin case, that the bobbin is inserted into the bobbin space correctly.
- Examine the needle to see if it is blunt or bent. If in doubt, replace it. Check that the needle is the right size and type and is inserted correctly in the machine.
- If your sewing machine requires regular oiling make sure you do it. Refer to the manual to see where oil should go and how regularly it should be applied.

3 Machine Embroidery Basic Skills

Machine-embroidered sample heart

Using a sewing machine for freestyle machine embroidery is different from general machine sewing, i.e. dressmaking or curtain making, etc. The main difference is that you work with the feed dog lowered, so you direct where the stitch line goes and not the feed dog (see 'Sewing machines' on page 13).

You use the sewing machine as a tool to 'paint with threads' and this way of working will soon become very familiar and natural so don't worry if it seems complicated or awkward at first. The more you embroider the easier it will become; confidence in your sewing machine and your own creativity will follow.

Making a sample heart

This project incorporates basic techniques which will be used in the various 'Projects to make', starting on page 75. The finished size is 4 x 5 cm (1½ x 2 in.).

YOU WILL NEED
Items from the 'basic tools' list on page 11 and the following materials:

- Heavyweight calico measuring 30.5 x 30.5 cm (12 x 12 in.)
- Machine embroidery thread or machine thread in 30 or 40 weight, in red, blue and black
- Stabilising fabric measuring 8 x 8 cm (3¼ x 3¼ in.)
- Five hand embroidery threads in red, blue and three other colours of your choice.

GETTING STARTED
Step 1
Insert a size 12/80 needle into your sewing machine. Fit the embroidery/darning foot to your machine and lower the feed dog. Adjust the tension bar to 'ordinary sewing' mode.

Step 2
Insert the calico in the embroidery hoop: Place the outer hoop (with the screw loosened) on a table. Lay the calico over it and place the other hoop over the top so that both hoops slot together with the calico sandwiched in the middle. Use a screwdriver to carefully tighten the hoop screw. Lay the hoop down with the calico side of the hoop on the table. Hold it with one hand and with the thumb and index finger of your other hand, pull the outside fabric taut all the way round.

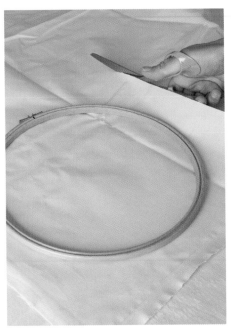

Cut the calico to fit the hoop
using sharp scissors

Place the calico in the hoop
and slot the inner hoop inside

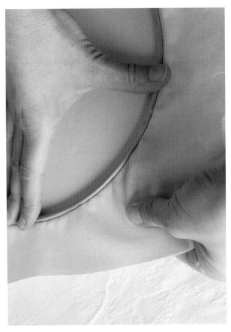

Hold the hoop firmly with one hand and
with the other pull the calico taut

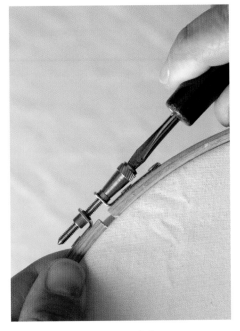

Use a screwdriver to carefully
tighten the hoop screw

Step 3

Wind a bobbin and thread the machine with black thread. Place the calico-filled embroidery hoop under the darning foot of the sewing machine, making sure that the needle is high and out of the way. Bring up the bobbin thread from underneath and through the calico by gently holding the top thread in your left hand and with your right hand turning the sewing machine wheel towards you until the needle goes down into the fabric. Keep turning the wheel towards you and when the needle comes back out of the calico gently pull on the top thread with your left hand. The bobbin thread will come up from underneath the calico. This action prevents the bobbin thread from jamming underneath. This step needs to be repeated every time you begin embroidering.

Step 4

Pull the two threads until they are about 20 cm (8 in.) long. Hold them with your left hand out of the way of the foot and needle and turn the wheel towards you again until the needle is back in the calico at the point where you want to start embroidering. Lower the presser foot.

Step 5

Hold either side of the hoop whilst still holding the two threads. Place your foot on the pedal and as you gently press, move the hoop away from you. You may experience an optical illusion of the needle coming towards you, but of course it stays in the same position and just goes up and down. By pushing the hoop away from you slightly a stitch line is created. The faster you push and pull the hoop the bigger the stitch you create. It is best to perform this task slowly at first until you gain confidence with the process and can produce at a faster pace. Apply pressure to the hoop to keep it flat as you sew. Draw a heart shape of about 3 x 2 cm (1¼ x ¾ in.) with the needle and thread of the sewing machine.

It is good practice to draw directly with the sewing machine in this way. However, if you do not feel confident enough to do this, draw a heart shape with the fabric drawing pen and follow the drawn line with the needle of the sewing machine.

Step 6

When the outline of your heart has been drawn in thread, cut off the two waste threads close to the embroidery. The stitches will not come undone because they are small and close together. Wind a bobbin and thread the machine with red thread. Using a vertical running stitch, fill in the heart with stitches in a backwards and forwards motion, treating the stitching as if you were shading

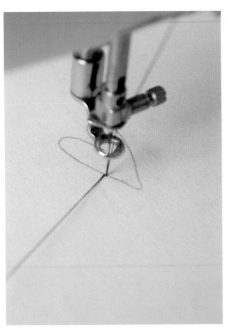

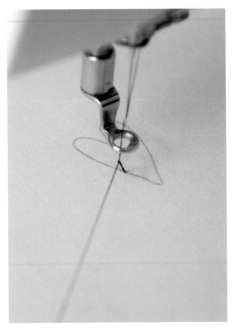

Lower the needle into the calico at the point where you will start stitching

Bring up the bobbin thread from underneath by turning the sewing machine wheel towards you

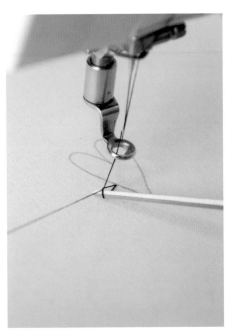

Use the points of your scissors to draw the bobbin thread through

Hold the waste threads away from your embroidery

Embroider the heart outline

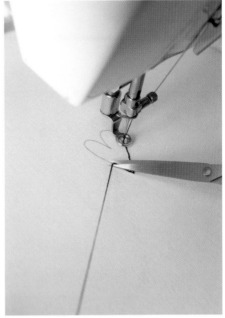

Cut off the waste threads

When the outline is complete, cut off the
waste threads on both front and back

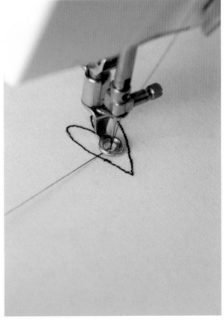

Start to fill in the heart with red thread

in with a pencil. You are now machine embroidering! It doesn't matter if you go over the initial outline of the heart shape as you can cover up any stray red stitches when you apply the background colour.

Step 7

Once the heart is filled with stitching, stop sewing, take your foot off the pedal and turn the machine wheel towards you until the needle is high and out of the way. Cut off the top thread close to the embroidered heart and pull the hoop away from the machine. Turn the hoop over and cut off the bobbin thread close to the embroidery.

Step 8

Remove the red thread from the machine and the bobbin. Wind another bobbin and thread the sewing machine with blue thread and repeat the whole process to work on the background. Draw a square of stitches around the heart measuring approximately 4 x 5 cm (1½ x 2 in.) or draw the outline with the fabric pen if you prefer. Embroider the background in the same way as for the heart and when complete cut off the top and bottom thread close to the stitching.

Have a good look at what you have embroidered and admire your work. Don't be too critical as this is your first piece of embroidery and you should be proud of your achievement.

Step 9

Take the fabric out of the hoop by loosening the screw and lay your embroidery piece upside down on an ironing board. With a hot steam iron, gently iron the back of your embroidered heart. NB: Check that the threads will not melt before you begin ironing.

FINISHING WITH A BORDER AND A TWIST OF HAND EMBROIDERY THREADS
Step 10

Keep the size 12/80 needle and the same colour thread used for the background in the sewing machine. Fit the ordinary sewing foot onto the machine, keep the tension set at 'ordinary sewing', and raise the feed dog. Change the stitch regulator to a wide zigzag and alter the stitch depth to a satin stitch effect (i.e. stitches very close together). Practise this stitch on a waste piece of fabric until you are happy with the quality of it.

Cut off the waste red threads

Fill in the heart with embroidery

Stop sewing when all the calico in the heart has been covered

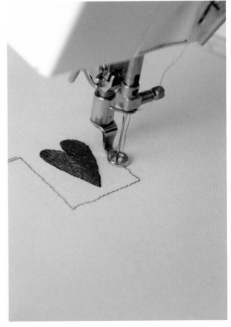

Draw an outline around the heart with blue thread

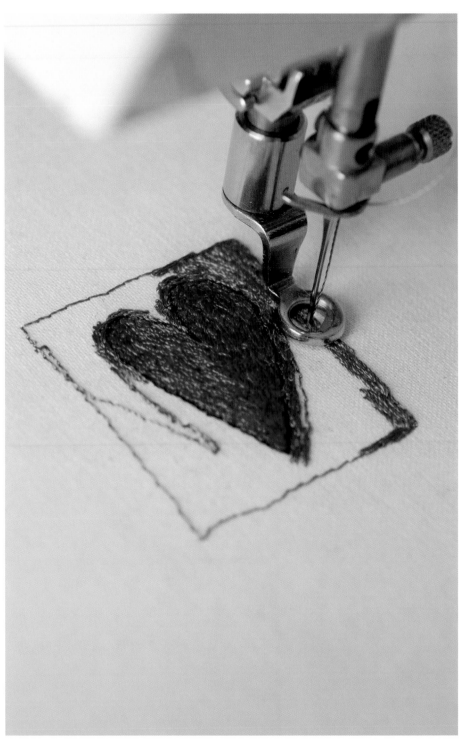

Fill in with the blue thread

Step 11

Cut the embroidery out of the calico leaving a border of about 5 mm (¼ in.). Place the piece onto the stabilising fabric, which has been cut to approximately 3 cm (1¼ in.) larger all round than the embroidery.

Step 12

Sew satin stitch around the outside of your embroidered heart twice. To do this, raise the feed dog, place the heart under the machine needle and start stitching at approximately 1 cm (½ in.) from the bottom right-hand side. The needle should catch the outside edge of the embroidery and be taken over to the stabilising fabric. Sew satin stitch to the end of the first side (the bottom side) to reach the first corner. Rotate the piece at the corner by 90 degrees and sew along the second side to the next corner and so on until you reach the last side. Pause sewing and leave the needle in the satin stitch. Cut off the threads at the beginning of the first side (bottom) before continuing to sew until you reach where you first began. Go over that and around the entire outside edge once more. Sew just a little over where you first began and stop with the needle raised. Pull the piece away from the machine and cut off the threads close to the stitching.

Step 13

Remove the stabilising fabric from the sample heart piece by gently tearing it away or, if necessary, cutting it away

Cut the sample heart piece from the calico leaving a border of about 5 mm (¼ in.)

Cut a piece of stabilising fabric approximately 3 cm (1¼ in.) bigger than the embroidery

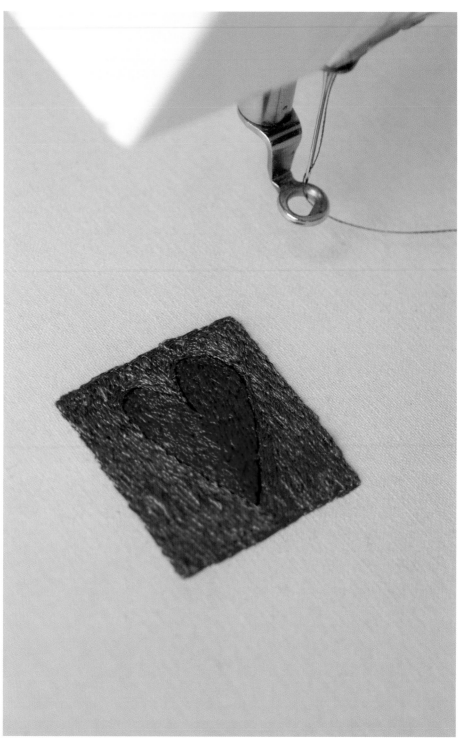

Finished blue background

Sew satin stitch around the edge
of the heart

Stitch around the edge twice and then
cut off all the waste threads

Tear away the stabilising fabric

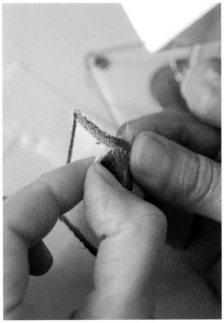

Remove the stabilising fabric from the back

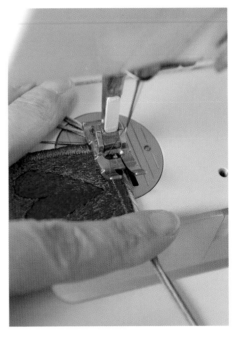

Carefully trim away any 'whiskers' of stabilising fabric

Place the twist of hand embroidery threads along the edge of the satin stitch border

Catch both sides of the corners

Cut off the waste twist threads

Sew over the twist a second time

Pull out and cut off the long threads

with a sharp pair of scissors, being careful not to cut any of the satin stitching. Don't worry too much if you can't remove all the little 'whiskers' from the piece as they will be covered when you finish off with the twist of hand embroidery threads.

Step 14

Now alter the zigzag stitch, keeping it wide but changing the depth to a more open stitch (i.e. the zigzag stitch that is used on a fabric edge to stop it from fraying). Lower the feed dog and place the heart under the foot of the sewing machine in the same place that you started and finished the satin stitch edge, slightly in from the bottom right-hand side.

Using sharp scissors, cut the twist remains close to the edge

Using a hand needle, sew the waste threads into the back of the twist

Step 15

Twist together the three hand embroidery threads and lay them along the bottom edge of the heart (they do not need to be cut to particular lengths as they can sit in your lap). Ensure the ends of the machine threads are out of the way. The aim is for the needle to catch the middle of the satin stitch and go over to the other side of the hand embroidery thread twist. Sew three or four zigzag stitches over the twist to hold them in place, making sure the needle also goes into the satin stitch border. Raise the feed dog and begin zigzag stitching carefully over the twist, remembering to always catch the needle into the satin stitch border. Continue to stitch along the bottom side until you reach the first corner and stop with the needle in the corner of the border.

Step 16

Lower the feed dog. Take the zigzag stitch over three or four times to catch the side of the corner, stop with the needle in the satin stitch border, lift the presser foot and turn the piece 90 degrees. Lower the presser foot again and take the zigzag stitch over the other side of the corner three or four times, catching the twist on this side. Raise the feed dog and continue to stitch, repeating the

Finishing the sample heart

procedure until you are working on the last side. Stop with the needle in the border and tuck the long machine threads under the heart to keep them out of the way, and continue stitching to the last corner. Complete as you did before and stitch over where you first started. Lower the feed dog and carry the stitch over three or four times, enough to secure the end of the twist. Raise the needle and presser foot, and pull out the machine threads and cut them to a length of 20 cm (8 in.).

Step 20

Cut the twisted embroidery threads close to the border, being careful not to cut the machine threads otherwise the twisted border may unravel. Using a hand sewing needle, sew the four long machine threads into the back of the border to secure them, and then cut off the waste thread close to the back of the border. Stand back and admire your beautiful sample heart!

4 Threads, Textures and Colour

The weight and thickness of the thread will determine whether you use it on the top of your sewing machine or in the bobbin. The two most popular weights of machine embroidery threads are 40 and 30 and both can be used on the top of the machine as well as in the bobbin. The 40 weight thread is thinner than a 30 weight and therefore takes more embroidering to fill up a space. However, it can give a fine stitch line when used singularly on delicate fabrics such as a

Girl and Seal by Linda Miller 2007
10 x 10 cm (4 x 4 in.)

thin silk. The 30 weight is a good all round thread, can easily fill in a large area and is suitable to use on both thick and thin fabrics. Most thread, whether machine embroidery or dressmaking machine thread, will have the weight and length of it printed on the label or on the spool.

Mixing colours

Threads can be used to create and mix colours, tones, weights and textures within your machine embroidery pieces. Here are a few suggestions:

Same thread on top and in bobbin – 30 weight

■ **True top thread colour** To embroider a block of one 'true' colour use the same colour and weight thread on the top of the machine as in the bobbin.

■ **Multi-coloured thread** Sometimes referred to as 'space-dyed thread', multi-coloured thread gives an instant marvellous effect, producing top colour changes in tone and shade as it is sewn. It need only be used on the top of the machine and any thread of the same weight and similar colour can be used in the bobbin.

Same thread on top and in bobbin – 40 weight

■ **Mixing bobbin and top threads** Using thread of the same weight, use one colour on the top of the machine and another in the bobbin. Choose similar or contrasting colours, depending on how subtle or dramatic you wish the effect to be. Tighten the top tension, which will draw the bobbin thread up from underneath to create little spots of colour in your embroidery.

Same thread on top and in bobbin – dressmaking thread

Multi-coloured thread

Mixing the bobbin thread
with the top thread

Mixing metallic bobbin thread
with the top thread

Metallic thread is particularly effective using this method as the spots sparkle. When you have finished, remember to reset the tension dial.

■ **Zigzag dots** To create little spots of colour on a flat colour surface of embroidery, first change the stitch to a very small zigzag, with a width of no more than 2 mm (1/10 in.) Choose a contrasting colour to that of the surface colour and lower the feed dog. With the embroidery hoop stationary, embroider a couple of zigzags. Raise the needle out of the embroidery and move the piece 1 cm (½ in.) or whatever distance you wish from the previous spots of colour, and repeat the process until all the desired spots of colour have been created. Lastly, cut off all the waste threads that have been carried from one area of spots to the next.

Metallic thread

Metallic thread gives sparkle and shimmer to an embroidered piece but it can at first be a little difficult to use due to its composition. However, the effects it can create are sumptuous and can add twinkling allure to an embroidery piece. Use a machine needle suitable for metallic thread.

To fill in a small area of embroidery, use metallic thread on the top of the machine and a non-metallic thread of the same weight and similar colour tone in the bobbin. Unless the back of the piece will be on view, it is unnecessary to use a metallic thread in the bobbin.

If you want to fill a large area with metallic thread and are finding it difficult to work with, fill a bobbin with some metallic thread and on top of the machine use a thread of similar weight, colour and tone, but non-metallic. Take the piece you are working on out of the embroidery hoop and turn it upside down, place it back in the hoop to work on the back of the piece. The metallic thread will of course feature on the right side of the piece.

Metallic thread

Thick thread

Any thread that cannot be easily threaded through the eye of your sewing machine needle due to its bulk and can only be used in the bobbin, is considered to be 'thick' thread. Machine embroidery thick thread is much thicker than 30 and 40 weight thread and gives a wonderful texture, creating an almost three-dimensional effect. When it is used with a thinner, contrasting coloured thread, wonderful mixes can be created, adding depth and lustre.

Mixing thick thread with 30 weight thread (thick thread in the bobbin and 30 weight thread on the top, worked on the back)

To use thick thread, wind it onto a bobbin spool either by hand or on the bobbin winder. Thread a 40 or 30 weight thread on the top of the machine, in either the same or a contrasting colour depending on the effect desired. Remove the embroidery piece from the hoop and turn the work upside down. Replace it in the hoop and carry on working on the back of the piece. As you sew, only the top 'thin' thread can be seen. Don't worry about filling up all the base fabric as the thick thread is doing this efficiently on the right side, underneath. When the desired amount of embroidering has been achieved, turn the piece right side up to reveal the thick thread effect with a lovely texture and colour mix.

To continue embroidering on the right side of the piece, take the fabric out of the hoop, turn it the right side up and return it to the hoop.

Two People and a Robin *by Linda Miller 2008 9 x 18 cm (3½ x 7 in.)*

5 Choosing Fabrics

As long as your sewing machine is able to cope with the thickness of the base fabric you can embroider onto almost any fabric. There is a wonderful variety available: plain, patterned, dark, light, natural and man-made. However, think about the type of project you will be working on and which fabric would be most suitable. For instance, it would be wasteful to use a piece of pure silk if you were going to cover the whole area in embroidery. Whereas if you were to use the same piece of silk and to embellish it with stitches, leaving unstitched areas, the silk, incorporated into the piece, would look stunning.

If you want your fabric to become sculptural as you embroider, use felt as your base fabric. As it is sewn onto, it moves and stretches due to the way it is manufactured, and you can create the most wonderful textured aspects.

If so desired, any fabric can be painted onto or dyed before you begin stitching. (You may need to wash the fabric first to remove any dressing to enable the dye to be absorbed into the fabric.) These techniques add instant colour, decoration and yet more intrigue to the base fabric if the surface is not solidly stitched.

Use stabilising fabric on the back of fine fabric to support dense stitching

Embroidery on this silk is supported by stabilising fabric on the reverse

The easiest and most popular base fabric to begin machine embroidering onto is a heavyweight calico. It is a natural material and not slippery or too fine. Calico is ideal for pictures and other pieces as it will remain relatively flat after all the base fabric has been stitched (as long as it is held firmly in an embroidery hoop). Being relatively inexpensive to buy and pale cream in colour, it is much easier to work on than a stark white fabric which can seem daunting.

Whatever base fabric you choose to work on – whether it is for a picture for your wall, a three-dimensional piece or an embellishment on a garment – once you have mastered the technique of freestyle machine embroidery you will have the confidence and ability to embroider on a whole range of different fabrics.

A delicate fabric such as silk or fine cotton incorporated into a picture or piece, but not solidly stitched onto, may need to have a stabilising fabric such as a lightweight (iron-on) Vilene ironed onto the back of it. This will help prevent the fine fabric from splitting and tearing as a result of dense machine stitching.

Stabilising fabric

If you want to embroider a motif or embellishment design onto a silk or a fine cotton garment, use a stabilising fabric such as 'stitch and tear'.
Place a piece of stabilising fabric on the 'wrong' side of the fabric to help prevent the delicate fabric from sheering away. A stabilising fabric is also used when finishing off pieces using the edging technique as shown in 'Making a sample heart' on p.21. It is much easier to obtain a clean zigzag line when a piece of stabilising fabric is incorporated on the back of the piece, and if the embroidery happens to be small it makes handling much easier.

Soluble fabric

Water soluble 'vanishing fabric' is great fun to use. Cold water soluble fabric is see-through and stretchy, which can take a little time to get used to, but it is easy to embroider onto. However, because of the compound of the material it can tear easily, so be careful when putting it into the embroidery hoop. Sometimes it can be easier to work with if it is folded in half and used double thickness. As you embroider your motif or design, ensure that each stitch overlaps the previous and the next one. If any gaps are left in the chain of stitches the embroidery will come undone in the finishing-off process. Once embroidering is completed, the vanishing fabric is washed away using warm water, leaving nothing but the motif, which has become three dimensional. The design could then be sewn onto a two-dimensional machine embroidery piece to create a free-standing embellishment. Some residue may be left behind in the stitching which makes the piece slightly sticky and this enables it to be moulded into a desired shape to give the motif more form. However, when it is completely dry it will have lost all stickiness and will be quite firm.

Soluble fabric

Place the soluble fabric into the hoop

Keeping the soluble fabric taut in the hoop, bring up the bobbin thread

Embroider your motif

Cut away any waste threads *Cut the embroidery from the soluble fabric*

Wash the fabric away in lukewarm water

Dry the embroidery before you use it

Running and Laughing *by Linda Miller 2008 19 x 41 cm (7½ x 16¼ in.)*

6 Finding Inspiration

A valuable tool and an excellent way to retain ideas is to keep a small notebook or sketchbook nearby as inspiration can strike at any time. We are surrounded by potential stimulus whatever we do, from gazing out of the kitchen window when washing the dishes, or strolling through a beautiful landscape on a country walk. Whether it is consciously or not, we constantly gather information and ideas from the world around us, some of which may appear in our creative work. It is often surprising what does appear when creating designs; thoughts and ideas are all found in our own unique and individual way. What we have seen, imagined, dreamt, and heard can all add to the rich tapestry of sourcing for work and projects.

It is easy to find ideas for current projects and future pieces. Think about what inspires and what interests you. We can visit galleries, museums, parks and gardens. There is an abundance of ideas and reference material to find in the world around us, for example from the internet, images cut from magazines, our own drawings, pictures and photographs of textures, patterns, shapes, landscapes and still life objects. Postcards old or new, whether depicting art or

Gardener by Linda Miller 2007 28 x 18 cm (11 x 7¼ in.)

a holiday destination sent by a friend, could all be glued into your sketchbook. Phrases that you may have heard in passing, whether in the Post Office queue or at a bus stop, can easily be scribbled down so they are ready and waiting to be used for a project. Sketchbooks are such a valuable resource when they are bursting with our gathered ideas, and creating them is a wonderful way to improve our ways of looking, seeing and recording.

Ideally, a drawing or sketch should be made each day but sometimes with our busy lives that is impossible, so draw and record when you can. Evenings, weekends and holiday times are all marvellous opportunities to record thoughts and ideas. Friends and family members are ideally captured when watching television, reading a newspaper or book, or relaxing in front of the fire on winter evenings. The television keeps people wonderfully still and occupied, unaware they are being studied, enabling us to draw them looking natural. When out and about sitting in cafes and parks, quick drawings can be made of other people enjoying a sit down and a coffee.

Supermarkets and shops are full of patterns, design and style, and whether they are to our taste or not, they are nevertheless full of interesting visual material; and we visit them so often. Next time you go, look at the way the tins are displayed with the labels facing forward. If you squint they could almost be a patchwork quilt of decorative fabric, and perhaps the same could be said for the neat rows of the brightly coloured plastic bottles? Use your imagination and enjoy the colours, textures, patterns, and all the free ideas for your own artwork.

The next time you are on a walk in the countryside stop for a few minutes to sketch the scene before you. Nature is on hand 24 hours a day, seven days a week with a constant changing and developing array of inspiration and source material. The whole panoply of nature is a wonderful cascade of every colour, texture and sense we could ever possibly imagine, and it is there for us to delve into at any time that suits us. We can reap the benefit and reward our creativity by drawing and sketching the landscape or sticking a leaf of the most awe-inspiring colour imaginable into our sketchbook. It is a good opportunity to practise drawing; your sketches will improve and your confidence will grow with each attempt.

Taking photographs is an instant way to capture a particular moment of inspiration. A digital camera is a wonderful quick visual tool to use, with the picture ready to look at as soon as it is taken.

Riverside Picnic by Linda Miller 2005 22 x 28 cm (8¾ x 11 in.)

Even if you can only go occasionally, visiting exhibitions and museums is such a joy and can be an invaluable experience. Everything from the ambience of the building, whether a small privately owned craft shop or a large public building, all adds to the visual experience. To be actually face to face with a painting, a piece of sculpture or an ancient piece of textile is even more rewarding than seeing a photo of it. To see all the brush strokes, chisel marks and stitch lines up close is awe-inspiring. It is also heartening to see what other artists, craftspeople and designers have been making throughout the year, years and centuries – their approach to the subject, how they made the object and the mediums used; the history behind the piece, the beauty contained within it, and the sheer love of making it. Whether purely to be admired by the viewer or made for practical reasons, knowing that a fellow human being had the desire and the urge to make objects just as we want to, can be enormously stimulating and encouraging.

Visiting exhibitions with a friend, where you can choose to enter into a discussion on what you have seen and whether or not you enjoyed it is an important exercise in ways of looking and seeing. Our sociable and enquiring human natures demand that we be constantly stimulated both mentally and visually. Whatever your reaction, think about and discuss it. This does not have to be an

Honey by Linda Miller 2004 30 x 21 cm (11¾ x 8¼ in.)

intellectual exercise, but it is important for our creative souls to engage in such matters and to listen to other opinions. Whether we agree with or challenge the debate, it allows us to gain a little more knowledge and understanding of what we are looking at as well as what we think about it. It all adds to the make-up of who we are and our standing in the world.

If you are unable to visit galleries and museums physically you can take a virtual tour of them and see some of the collections via the internet. Only a couple of key words need to be entered into a search engine and the whole of the world wide web is available. If you do not have your own computer, you can use one at your local library – most town libraries provide this service now and often have helpful librarians on hand to guide the novice computer user.

We are lucky we have everything we need to hand, ready to use. Food for the soul!

Influence versus copying

The whole point of opening our minds to the world around us in relation to creativity is to be influenced by it. There can sometimes be a fine line between being influenced by another artist's work and copying it, so it is vital that you get permission from them before using their ideas in your own work. It is good professional practice to respect the ideas of others and for each of us to create our own unique ones.

Beach Cagools *by Linda Miller 2008 9 x 18 cm (3½ x 7 in.)*

7 Using Imagery

As applies to so many things, keep it simple. Remember that 'less is more' and do not overcomplicate your design. Due to the nature of the process and the fact that there is much dense stitching in a small area, solidly stitched machine embroidery can at times become quite stiff and 'heavy' to work on. So without compromising your design and skill, use these elements to your advantage and keep your initial design simple. It will free you to concentrate on the concise design that you have. Once all the sewing has been completed you can always give your piece extra embellishment with beads, buttons, tassels, or whatever you wish, but keep the thought 'less is more' in mind.

Study the elements involved and the composition of your source material before you draw as you may wish to alter aspects. For example, if you have taken a photograph of a landscape which you wish to translate into a machine embroidery scene, there may be parts of the composition that you really like and other elements that you feel do not work as well. As the artist, you decide what elements of the reference material to keep and what to take away. There is no wrong or right way; it is down to an individual perspective and how the artist chooses to place the imagery. Sometimes you may find that a piece works better if the 'main object' or the most important item of the piece is not positioned in the middle of the design, but situated slightly to the right or left. A landscape could be more intriguing as a design if the tree – the 'important item' – is situated, say, to the right of the composition. The same could be said for the horizontal line where the foreground meets the background. Rather than having the horizon in the middle of your design, try positioning it either slightly up (reducing the sky area) or slightly down (increasing the amount of sky). Try out different compositions and see what you prefer.

Do not compromise this stage of the process. If you are not entirely satisfied with your drawing don't use it. It can be helpful to cut up the original drawing and reassemble it on a new piece of paper, as changing the initial design can create a whole new ambience to your idea, therefore creating another starting point. You need to be pleased and excited with your design before starting to embroider. Only use a drawing that you are truly happy with as you will spend a lot of time and energy working on it. Be brave and rely on your creative instincts and be true to yourself for it will save you a lot of heartache in the long run.

You may need to do lots of drawing before you are satisfied with your design. You can use a photocopier, or copies of a drawing can be achieved very easily using a light box or window. Stick your drawing onto the window pane with low tack tape. Place and stick a piece of thin paper over the top. The original drawing will show through and you can trace your drawing onto the top piece of paper. Photocopy it to either enlarge or reduce the size, or just to have more copies. You can draw purely in black and white or may choose to add colour to enhance parts of your design and to give you an idea of how the colours will work together when you begin to sew.

Autumn Leaves by Linda Miller 2008 11 x 15 cm (4½ x 6 in.)

8 Finishing Techniques

As suggested previously, do not overwork the embroidery in your piece and remember that 'less is more'. If your piece is pictorial there is only a certain amount of stitching that you can do until all the base fabric is filled and the picture is complete.

When making an abstract patterned piece it may be hard to know when the design can be considered finished, because there is no pictorial guidance within it. You do not want to reach the stage where you cannot continue sewing because the embroidery has become too thick and difficult to work on. Determining the amount of patterning and texture to apply without the piece

becoming too full and overworked can often only be achieved by stopping every so often to assess it. Physically stepping back to look at your work and perhaps leaving it for a few minutes or hours and thinking about something else are both helpful. On your return you will look upon it with a refreshed mind and be able to decide whether (and how) to continue or to begin the finishing-off process.

When you consider the embroidering process finished, the piece then needs to be edged and proffered for framing and presentation. Check that there are no stray threads on the front that need to be trimmed and neatened up. Similarly, tidy the back, even though it is unlikely the back will be on show.

After you have taken the piece out of the hoop, you may want to flatten the embroidery slightly using a steam iron, as the surface can become uneven as a result of dense stitching in different directions onto the base fabric. (NB: Check that the threads will not melt before you begin ironing.) However, if you choose to leave the surface as it is you can gain a pleasing amount of rich texture and embellishment within the piece.

Do not embellish with any hand stitching or accessories such as buttons, beads, sequins, etc. until the piece is completely finished, ironed and edged. It may be just right as it is, and by waiting until after ironing it you can be guaranteed that any extra three-dimensional decoration you use for embellishment will not melt and taint your hard work.

As you work on your design, and then the piece, both will change again and again: this is all part of the making process. Of course, sometimes it can be frustrating that we cannot control every part of the process and have it exactly as we want. This mindset can leave you feeling defeated and frustrated. However, do not be disheartened as sometimes it can be a welcome change, one that is exciting and inspiring, and move our work and ideas in directions that we had not considered before. From our original starting point so much more can be achieved and realised by the nature of the materials and equipment used and by engaging with our creativity.

When all the sewing of your piece has been accomplished you can consider how it should be finished off and edged. There are many different ways to finish the edges, and your choice depends on the type of work you have created.

A finished machine embroidery piece

After cutting the piece from the calico sew over the edge to finish it

First consider how the piece will be displayed. Is the edge of the piece an integral part of the display? Will the back of the work be on show? Do you want the edge of the piece to stand out or to blend in with the piece itself?

Incorporating the edge into the picture

You may want to take the machine embroidery to the edge of your piece without having a purpose-made edging to it. When the embroidering is finished, remove the piece from the hoop and cut away the base fabric to leave a base fabric border of no more than 5 mm (¼ in.). If the piece has an uneven edge you can decide whether to keep it so, which can add to the overall design and look to the piece, or to have the edges straight.

Then, holding the fabric taut in your hands and keeping it on the machine bed as much you can (so the edge of the fabric will not stretch too much, creating a ripple effect), continue to embroider to the edge and slightly beyond the base fabric. (NB: Be very careful to keep your fingers well away from the needle of the machine.) By taking the machine stitches over the edge of the fabric in a quick motion you will be guaranteed stitching right to the edge, therefore incorporating it into your picture.

Gluing the edges

Gluing is a very quick way of managing the edges of your piece without sewing, but the back of the work will not be as neatly presented as the front and it can be a bit messy to do.

When you have completed embroidering, take the piece out of the hoop and steam iron it if necessary. (If it is ironed after it has been glued it could cause a mess.) Cut away the waste base fabric to leave a hem of approximately 1–2 cm (½–¾ in.) around the outside of the work, depending on the size of it, to avoid the back of your piece having bulky turned-in edges.

Use good quality fabric glue. Test it first on some waste fabric and allow it to dry thoroughly to make sure it remains on the back surface of the embroidery and will not seep through to the front of your work to ruin it.

On the back of the piece apply glue sparingly onto the fabric hems and turn them in, pressing gently. Use clothes pegs to keep the hems in place until they are dry and secure.

Apply fabric glue carefully to the hem on the back of the piece

Hand sewing the edges

This is another quick (depending on the size of your piece) and simple way of turning over the edges, although the back of your work will not be as neatly presented as the front.

When the embroidering has been completed, remove the piece from the hoop and steam iron it, if desired. Cut away the waste base fabric to leave a hem of approximately 1–2 cm (½ – ¾ in.) around the piece, depending on the size of your work to avoid bulky turned-in edges. Cut away diagonally the tops of the corners of the base fabric edges 5 mm (¼ in.) from the embroidery edge, and turn under the hems to the back of the embroidery. It is not necessary to turn the hems twice as in dressmaking as once secured the fabric will not fray. Using dressmaking quality polyester thread in a colour that is similar to the majority of your piece, hand sew the hems. Make sure you avoid stitching through to the front of the piece.

Handsew the hem on the back of the piece

Edging with a machine satin stitch and a twist of threads

For a decorative and robust edge, using satin stitch with a twist of coloured hand-embroidery threads is an excellent technique to use. It is ideal for many machine embroidery project edges, e.g. glazed and unglazed framed pieces, jewellery pieces and three-dimensional vessels.

The satin stitch can be sewn in the same colour as the piece or in a contrasting colour to enhance and enliven it. Similarly, the twist of threads that lie at the outside edge of the satin stitch can include the colours used in the piece, or some that contrast with it. Possibly a little tricky to use initially, once mastered this technique can be used for a variety of projects. For instructions, see 'Making a sample heart' on page 21

A framed piece ready to be hung

9 Framing and Presenting Work

Framing your completed two-dimensional work finishes it off to a professional level, ready to be presented to the public.

It can be a daunting task to frame one's own work, having spent a long and concentrated time on it from the initial idea to its final realisation. Presenting it to its full and deserved potential is a skill, but one that can be achieved with thought and care.

There is a huge selection of frames available – from the plain and neutral to the highly decorative, stained and guilded – and what best suits your work can be a taxing choice. Textiles need to be set back from the glass, so a box style frame is required for your work.

You may prefer to hand the task over to a professional framer. If you do, choose one who is sympathetic towards stitched textiles. Sometimes it can be more convenient to have a professional and objective opinion on how best to execute and frame your work.

However, there is something very satisfying about seeing a project through to the very end, especially one that is so personal. If you want to frame your work yourself, do not be tempted by cheap mass-produced frames, especially clip frames, as they are rarely the best option. Cheap frames can make your work look as cheap. Having spent copious amounts of time and energy on your piece, it deserves to be presented at its very best.

Department stores, home interior stores and the internet can all offer good plain and simple frames as well as more decorative ones, which can complement your work well. Consider also looking in secondhand shops and at car boot sales; keep all your sourcing options open. Be selective and judge wisely. Also consider using an unglazed frame. To many enthusiasts this is the best way to present textiles as the viewer can see the whole piece without it being distorted

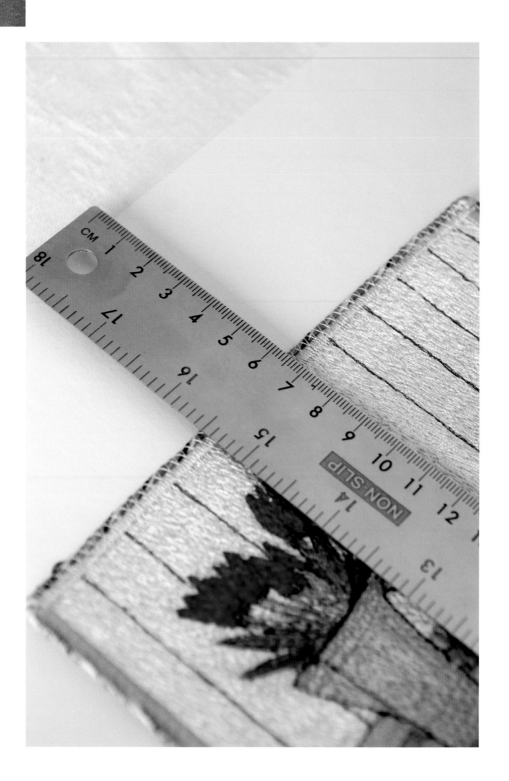

Position and measure your piece on the mountboard

by glass. However, there is always the concern that the piece will fade quicker or get damaged more easily.

As with all art and crafts, textiles need to be respected and some of the ways to do this are:

- Keep them away from direct sunlight
- Keep them away from humidity and within reason at a steady temperature
- Minimise the acid environment which they are housed in, and when mounting textiles use acid-free mountboard.

The ideal frame should be neither too big nor too small for the work; should enhance the image and draw the viewer's eye to it; and it should complement and promote the piece, but never dominate it.

Use pliers and a thick hand sewing needle to make the holes through the mountboard

However you choose to frame your work, the best way to prepare it for hanging is to attach D-rings and picture cord to the back of the frame structure. D-rings are named after their shape, and attached to the back of the frame by a hinged piece of metal with screw holes. Make sure that the cord is strong enough to take the weight of the picture and frame before hanging it on the wall.

The space around the piece of work should be between approximately 7–11 cm (2¾–4½ in.). Ideally, the dimensions around the top and two sides of the image should be the same, and the space at the bottom slightly bigger.

If your piece looks lost or squashed, try it on another piece of card that is either smaller or bigger and see how it looks. You could ask for a second opinion from someone whose judgement you trust.

Securing a textile piece onto mountboard

When you are happy with the size of the mountboard, the embroidery piece needs to be secured to it by either gluing or sewing. If you opt for glue, use a good quality textile-friendly glue, as described in 'Finishing techniques' (page 57).

Sewing down the piece takes longer but has its advantages. It avoids the possibility of a gluey mess, and if the piece does not sit properly or needs to be moved, all you need do is snip the holding stitches and reposition it. This can be easier than picking off and tidying up bits of glue, but in some projects glue is a more appropriate option. Sewing the piece onto mountboard needs to be done by hand; a sewing machine is likely to struggle with the thickness.

Run the strong hand sewing thread through beeswax before using it

First place a cutting mat onto a table or other stable surface with an old thick blanket folded into quarters (to give it some extra thickness) on top of it. Put the mountboard and textile piece on top of the blanket and with a large, sharp, hand sewing needle held in a pair of pliers, press the needle through the corner of the piece of work a couple of millimetres in from the edge and push down hard so that the needle goes all the way through the piece and mountboard. Make another hole 1 cm (½ in.) along from the first. Move the pliers and needle along about 3–4 cm (1¼–1¾ in.) and make another hole, then another one 1 cm (½ in.) away from that. Continue in this way until marker holes have been made all around the piece.

If the piece is very thick you may only be able to mark the mount board, but once all the marks have been made you can lift the piece out of the way and push the needle through the marks to make the desired holes.

Push the needle through the mountboard

Catch the back of the embroidery with the needle and thread

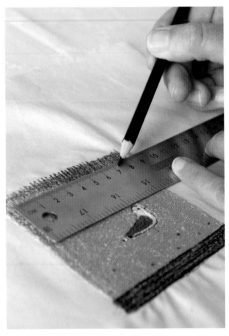

Pull the thread tight on the back of the mountboard and knot

Measure the piece to determine how big to cut the window mount

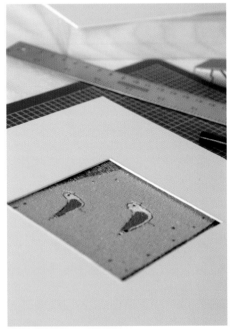

Cut the window mount

A window mounted piece ready for its frame

Thread a hand sewing needle with some strong thread in a colour that is neutral to the main colour in your piece. Pull the thread through some beeswax to make it easier to sew with. Start sewing the top right-hand corner onto the mount board by pushing the needle through the back of the board and catch the back of the piece. Try not to go all the way through so that the embroidery stays neat on the right side. Push the needle through the next hole and pull the thread to leave about 8 cm (3¼ in.), which is enough to make a reef knot. Tie off the loose end.

Push the needle through the next hole (3–4 cm/1¼–1¾ in. along), once again catching the back of your embroidery piece. Press the needle through the next hole and pull the thread tight and knot it on the back, taking the needle under the large stitch just made, then going back through the loop and pull. Do this twice to create a knot and so secure the back. Continue sewing and knotting along the top and down the left-hand side, then stop when you reach the bottom left-hand corner. Knot and cut off the waste thread. As you sew keep measuring in order to keep the piece in the desired place on the mount board and check that it is straight.

Then start the whole sewing process again from the top right-hand corner down the right side and along the bottom, finishing at the bottom left-hand corner. Knot and cut off the waste sewing thread. Your piece is now ready to be framed.

Sew the fabric tube onto the back of the piece

Screw the eyes to each end of the wooden pole

Window mounts

If you have not embroidered solidly on all the base fabric in your piece, it may be desirable to simply cut a window mount out of good quality acid-free mount board. Choose either a neutral colour or one that complements the piece. Place it over the design and frame it accordingly, deciding if you want a border of base fabric around the picture or not. Having a couple of window mounts around the piece adds depth, so that when everything is placed in the frame the glass rests on the mount board and not the embroidery. Alternatively, you can omit the mount board and frame the piece with a border of the base fabric showing in the frame. However, be aware that textiles attract moisture, so ensure none of the piece touches the glass.

Unframed and free-hanging wall pieces

There are occasions when the only solution to the final presentation of your piece is to leave it unframed. Sometimes the piece can look just right as it is, and nothing else can enhance or complement it any further; adding more would simply complicate it. If the piece is very large it may not suit, or need, a frame and looks complete by itself.

Screw the hooks near to the ends of the wooden wall baton and drill two holes into the baton ready to attach to the wall

The simplest way to display a free-standing wall piece is to have it suspended from a pole which has been inserted into a fabric tube sewn

The free-hanging piece. Forest Dream *by Linda Miller*
1997 70 x 98 cm (27½ x 38¾ in.)

to the back of the piece. First, make sure that the edges are tidy, any loose threads are trimmed, and if desired, steam or lightly iron the piece.

Take a length of fabric about 8cm (3¼ in.) shorter than the width of the piece and deep enough to have a pole inserted into it when sewn into a tube. Then hand sew the tube onto the back of the piece at the top, leaving a gap of 4cm (1¾ in.) in from each side and 2–3cm (¾–1¼ in.) from the top. As you sew, periodically check that when the pole is inserted into the tube the piece hangs straight as you may need to sew the tube on at a slight angle to compensate for the irregular hang.

After the pole has been inserted, screw two metal eyes into each end. Take a piece of wood 2.5–5cm (1–2 in.) wide, depending on the size and weight of the embroidery, and slightly longer than the pole, and attach it to the wall for the pole to hang from. Secure two metal hooks to it, protruding at an equivalent distance to the two pole eyes. The piece can now be hung.

Using the techniques and guidelines given previously, instructions for five machine embroidery projects follow in the next chapter:

- A picture of your own design
- Jewellery pieces
- A keepsake box
- A needle case
- A photo frame.

10 Projects to Make

All the projects require the same basic tools listed on page 11 and, in addition, each project has a unique list of materials listed at the start of each project.

To begin the machine embroidery process in each of these projects please refer to 'Making a sample heart' on page 21.

When you use your sewing machine for embroidery you must have the compatible embroidery/darning foot correctly fitted and the feed dog lowered.

With each new project fit a new needle to your machine, and dispose safely of the old one.

When you need to re-thread your machine or use a different colour/type of thread, follow the process described in 'Making a sample heart' on page 21 to ensure trouble-free embroidering. After changing threads, bringing up the bobbin thread, and cutting the waste threads close to the embroidery (when starting and finishing off) a few times, the whole process will seem like second nature.

The sewing machine tension setting for all the projects is 'ordinary sewing' unless otherwise stated. Depending on your machine tension and the weight and type of thread, the finished size of your own project may be either slightly smaller or larger than that of the size stated by approximately 5 mm/¼ in. This is quite normal as everybody sews differently and machine embroidery always changes size as it is sewn.

Tools and materials

A picture of your own design

Make an embroidered 'still life' picture taken from your own original drawing. The finished size of the embroidered picture (not including the frame) is approximately 12 x 17 cm (4¾ x 6¾ in.).

YOU WILL NEED

Items from the 'basic tools' list plus:

- Heavyweight calico measuring 32 x 32 cm (12½ x 12½ in.)
- Stabilising fabric measuring 23 x 18 cm (9 x7 in.)
- A ready-to-use box-style frame suitable for wall-hanging, measuring 30 x 24 cm (12 x 9½ in.)
- All the frame components
- A piece of pale cream mount board to fit snugly into the back of the frame
- Pliers
- Cutting mat
- An old thick blanket
- Embroidery/ordinary sewing machine threads in 30 or 40 weights in the colours of:
  black – outlines
  pale blue – jug
  forest green – flower stems
  multi-coloured green – flower stems and apple leaves
  periwinkle blue – background stripes
  white – inside of the bowl
  red – outside of the bowl pattern
  yellow – outside of the bowl pattern
  cobalt blue – outside of the bowl pattern
  pale yellow – background
  orange – table mat border
  lime green – apples
  grey – table mat
  multi-coloured pink – dots on the tablecloth
  oatmeal – tablecloth
  turquoise – patterned border on the table mat
  dark brown – apple stalks
- Red thick thread for the flowers

- Six hand embroidery threads in the colours of: cobalt blue, yellow, turquoise, red, orange and forest green (these colours are recommendations; feel free to choose different ones)
- Strong hand-sewing thread
- Beeswax.

In addition, you will require some objects for the still life setup, such as a jug, red flowers, a bowl, a decorative mat, a tablecloth and green apples. Arrange them on a tabletop with either a coloured wall or a length of coloured fabric behind. You can try a simple patterned backdrop, but avoid it being too bold as you want to concentrate on the still life rather than have a dominating background.

When you select the thread colours for your picture, have some neutral or pale colours as well as bright ones. Your piece needs to have good contrast so use bolder colours for the objects to ensure they stand out.

Draw your still life

GETTING STARTED

Place the items on the tabletop and rearrange them until you are happy with the composition. Take two pieces of paper and on each of them draw a rectangle measuring 12 x 17 cm (4¾ x 6¾ in.). This is the size of your drawing and the approximate size of the finished piece. The nature of dense stitching onto the fabric will cause the embroidery to reduce slightly in size from the original drawing. However, you can increase the size when your picture is almost finished by stitching around each side.

In one of the rectangles sketch a rough drawing of the still life arrangement. Keep it simple. You can embellish and enrich your picture with decorative threads and colour mixes as you embroider later on. As the artist, have the confidence to draw in your own unique way to capture how you see the still

Draw the image onto the calico

life. When you are happy with the sketch, trace it onto the other piece of paper using the light box/window pane technique as described on page 56. With the sketch as a template, redraw the still life using simple clear lines and bold shapes to simplify your design. To get it how you want, feel free to move the objects and height of the table at this stage. You may find it easier to cut out the sketched items with a pair of scissors and collage them onto another piece of paper. Continue to rearrange them until you are happy with the arrangement, then stick them down using either a glue stick or translucent sticky tape. Using coloured pencils, you can depict the design either in the original colours of the still life or reinvent them.

Stick your drawing onto the light box or window pane using a couple of pieces of masking tape, and stick the calico over the top of it. Using the fabric drawing pen, trace the drawing onto the fabric using clear lines.

Remove the tape from both the fabric and paper drawing and stick or pin the paper drawing onto a wall where you can see it from your sewing machine. This will be the original template and reference guide for your embroidery.

Outline your drawing in black thread

Begin to embroider, following the contours of the objects

Step 1

Place the piece of calico in the wooden embroidery hoop. Make sure your sewing machine is in embroidery mode and has an embroidery/darning foot fitted. Use black thread both on the top of the machine and in the bobbin. Stitch the calico, following the drawn pen lines with the needle to define the outlines of the objects for when you later embroider other threads onto the piece. When all the pen lines have been stitched, cut off the waste threads on the top and back of the piece close to the stitching.

Step 2

Re-thread the top of the machine and the bobbin with the colour you have chosen for the jug. It is much easier to embroider the 'important' items in a picture first, and in this case it is the still life objects.

Follow the shapes and contours of the still life items to give your picture form, substance and a three-dimensional feel to it as you embroider. For instance, embroider over your drawing of the jug in a vertical manner, and then embroider horizontally for the top of the handle and down again in a vertical motion for the handle arm, and so on, until the whole jug has been filled with stitching. Take the same approach for the apples, except this time follow the shape of the apples with a semi-circular motion to give them the appearance of being round. With the bowl, again take the stitches in a semi-circular direction, and for the mat and tabletop run the embroidery stitches horizontally. To separate the background from the foreground take the background stitches in a vertical direction, thus breaking up all the objects and giving them individual cast and essence.

Try to keep within the black outlines as much as you can, although if you do go over them you can cover up the stray stitches when you stitch the background colour.

If you look closely at an apple you will see that it has many subtle colours to it. To capture this effect, mix colours for the apples together by having a yellow thread in the bobbin and an apple green thread in the top of the machine. As described in 'Mixing colours' on page 39, tighten the top tension on the sewing machine to achieve little spots of yellow in the green, which give an interesting contrast of colour mixes. You could use the same technique for the bowl, especially if it has a pattern. This is a good way to break up flat areas and suggest to the viewer that it is more complicated than it really is, giving the whole picture more curiosity and depth.

Try out colour mixes on the 'waste' base fabric that surrounds the picture in the hoop. This 'waste' fabric can prove invaluable for experimenting with threads and colours before applying them to the actual embroidery as once you have embroidered onto the actual picture, it can be difficult and time consuming to unpick stitching if the effect is disappointing.

The flower heads could be embroidered using a thick thread, which would make them stand out and create a different texture within the picture (see 'Thick thread' on page 41). For the flower stems you could use a multi-coloured green thread to break up the colour of the stems.
Continue to embroider the still life objects, the foreground and the background

Spring stroll by Linda Miller 2008 19 x 22 cm (7½ x 8¾ in.)

of your picture, remembering to stitch in different directions. Make sure you cut off the waste threads close to the embroidery on the front and back when you are ready to change and re-thread the machine in a different colour to keep stray threads at bay and leave a tidy finish. When all the base fabric of the picture has been covered and you are happy with the amount of stitching achieved, stop sewing and take a good look at your picture.

Step 3

If there are any fine details that you are not confident to machine stitch, you can hand sew them. If you want to add any three-dimensional embellishments such as beads and buttons, wait until the piece is completely finished and there is no chance of melting them with a hot iron or catching them as you edge and finish off the piece.

Step 4

Cut off any waste threads and take the piece out of the embroidery hoop. It is now ready to be steam ironed to flatten it slightly if you wish.

This picture project has been designed to go into a frame so think carefully how you want to finish off the edges. Choose one of the edging methods from 'Finishing techniques' (page 57) and consider how you wish to frame your picture from one of the methods described in 'Framing and presenting work' (page 65).

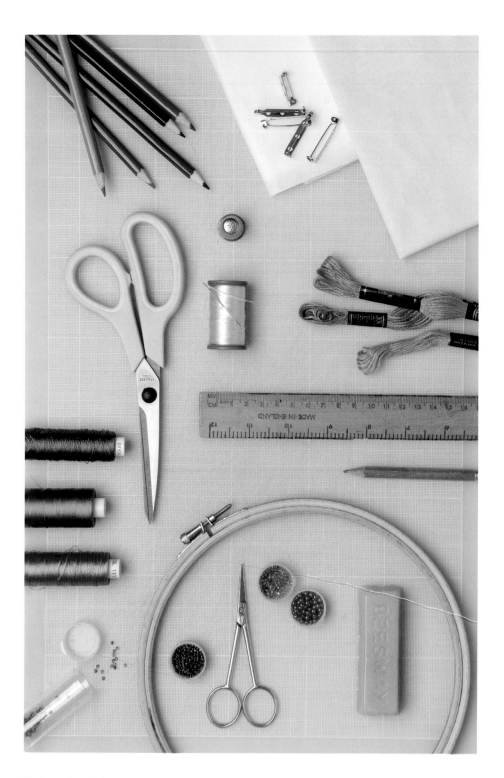

Tools and materials

Jewellery pieces

Brighten up a shirt or jacket with an embroidered brooch and make a pair of earrings to match! The initial design idea was taken from a daisy, which was then simplified into a daisy-style motif and decorated and embellished with glass beads. The finished size of the brooch, including beads, is 5 x 5 cm (2 x 2 in.) and of the earrings, including beads, is 3.5 x 3.5 cm (1½ x 1½ in.).

YOU WILL NEED
Items from the 'basic tools' list plus:

- Heavyweight calico measuring 30.5 x 30.5 cm (12 x 12 in.)
- Stabilising fabric measuring 23 x 18 cm (9 x 7 in.)
- Small glass beads in the colours of: periwinkle blue, lime green and cerise pink
- Three hand embroidery threads in the colours of: periwinkle blue, lime green and cerise pink
- Beading thread
- Beading needle
- Beeswax
- A brooch fastening no bigger than 2 cm (¾ in.) in length (with holes in the bar so it can be sewn to the brooch)
- Stud earring fastenings
- Strong glue such as epoxy resin adhesive
- Embroidery/ordinary machine sewing threads in either 30 or 40 weights in:
black – for outlines
  - periwinkle blue – daisy motif
  - lime green – background
  - cerise pink – daisy centres.

GETTING STARTED
In the centre of a piece of paper draw round a 2.5 cm (1 in.) coin for the brooch and draw twice around a 2 cm (¾ in.) coin for the earrings, and then draw your daisy motif inside these circles. If you feel confident you can draw directly onto the calico. Stick the paper onto a light box or a window pane using a couple of pieces of masking tape and stick the piece of calico on top so that the coin templates show through in the middle of the calico. Using the fabric drawing pen, draw round the coins onto the calico using the paper as a template. You may need to do this twice in order to make the lines really bold and then draw the daisy motif in the circles.

Step 1

Fill a bobbin and thread the top of the machine with black thread. Put the calico in the embroidery hoop and tighten the screw, then pull the base fabric taut. Follow the daisy motif pattern with the needle on the brooch and two earring pieces until all the fabric pen lines have been covered with a black stitch line. Stop sewing and take the embroidery hoop away from the machine, cutting off the top and bottom threads close to the stitching.

Change the bobbin and re-thread the machine with the periwinkle blue thread. Embroider the petals starting in the middle and stitch outwards towards the tips, following the contours of the daisy shape. Leave the daisy centre un-embroidered as stitching over the top with the pink thread later will cause problems owing to the thickness of the embroidered surface.

Step 2

When all the desired embroidering has been achieved, take the hoop from under the sewing machine and cut off the waste thread on the front and back of the embroidery. Re-thread the machine and bobbin in the lime green thread and place the hoop back under the machine. Embroider the background, first following the petal outlines on the brooch piece. Then take the direction of your stitches in a vertical motion. This will keep the jewellery pieces lying relatively flat. Follow the same procedure for the earring pieces. Change the colour of the thread on top of the machine and in the bobbin to cerise pink and fill in the centre of the daisy on both the brooch and the earrings. Take the hoop out of the machine and cut away the threads close to the embroidery on the front and back. Then remove the calico from the hoop and place it upside down on an ironing board where you can steam iron the back. (NB: Be sure that your threads are heat-proof.)

Step 3

The pieces are now ready for edging. The most suitable method for these jewellery pieces is a satin stitch border finishing with a twist of hand embroidery threads, using the lime green thread as the edging colour.

Cut round the jewellery pieces using sharp scissors, leaving a calico border of about 5 mm (¼ in.) and place the pieces onto the stabilising fabric. Fit an ordinary sewing foot on your sewing machine, raise the dog feed and re-thread the machine in lime green. Follow the instructions for the edging technique

Jewellery pieces

Embroider the flower motif

as described in 'Making a sample heart' (page 21) using periwinkle blue, lime green and cerise pink hand embroidery threads. When the border technique is finished sew the strands of thread into the back of the brooch.

Beading the edges of the brooch

Thread the beading needle with beading thread and knot it at the end with a small, secure and discreet knot. Turn the brooch over and push the needle into the back of the border so that it comes out on the very edge of the brooch. Then thread the beads onto the beading needle in this order: six periwinkle blue, one lime green, one cerise pink, one lime green and six periwinkle blue. Push the beads down the thread as you add them until the first periwinkle blue bead is flush with the outside edge of the brooch, and all the others are in a tight line behind. Push the needle into the front of the brooch, just by the outside edge, about 1.5 cm (¾ in.) along from where the needle first came out, so creating a loop with the beads, and pull it out of the back. Then take the needle into the last three periwinkle blue beads, pulling it tight as you go to keep the loops secure and erect.

Now thread more beads onto the needle in this order: three periwinkle blue, one lime green, one cerise pink, one lime green and six periwinkle blue, pushing the beads down the thread as you go. Again, push the needle into the front of the brooch, just by the outside edge, about 1.5 cm (¾ in.) along from where the needle came out, making another loop with the beads. Push the needle all the way into the border once more and pull it out of the back, then up into the last three periwinkle blue beads, pulling it tight.

Repeat this procedure of creating bead loops around the edge of your brooch until you are 1.5 cm (¾ in.) away from the first loop of beads. Push the needle back into the front of the border just by the edge, and push it

Use glass beads to decorate the jewellery pieces

up through the three periwinkle blue beads. Put the last beads on the needle in this order: three periwinkle blue, one lime green, one cerise pink, one lime green and three periwinkle blue. Push the needle down into the last three periwinkle blue beads, into the top of the edge and out into the back of the border.

Secure the thread by backstitching into the back of the satin stitch border a few times. Then cut off the thread close to the back of the embroidery. Sew the brooch fastening onto the back of the brooch.

Beading the edges of the earrings

Thread the beading needle with the beading thread and make a small, discreet knot at the end. Turn the earring over and push the needle through the back on the satin stitch border so that it comes out on the very edge of the earring. Thread one periwinkle blue bead onto the needle and push it back into the edge of the earring next to the bead to secure it. Bring the needle out about 1 cm (½ in.) along from there, again on the very edge of the earring and place another periwinkle blue bead on the needle and push it back into the edge to secure it. Bring the needle back up to the very edge, again about 1 cm (½ in.) from the second bead, and continue until the last bead has been sewn in place about 1 cm (½ in.) in front of the first bead. As you progress, ensure you do not pull the beading thread too tightly, otherwise the edge of the earring will bunch up.

Bring the needle out of the back of the satin stitch border and sew a couple of backstitches to secure it. Cut off the thread close to the back of the embroidery. Complete the other earring in exactly the same way.

When both earrings have been beaded, stick the fastenings onto the back using strong glue. (Test the glue first on some waste embroidery to make sure that it will not seep through.)

Continue to bead the edge all the way round the jewellery piece

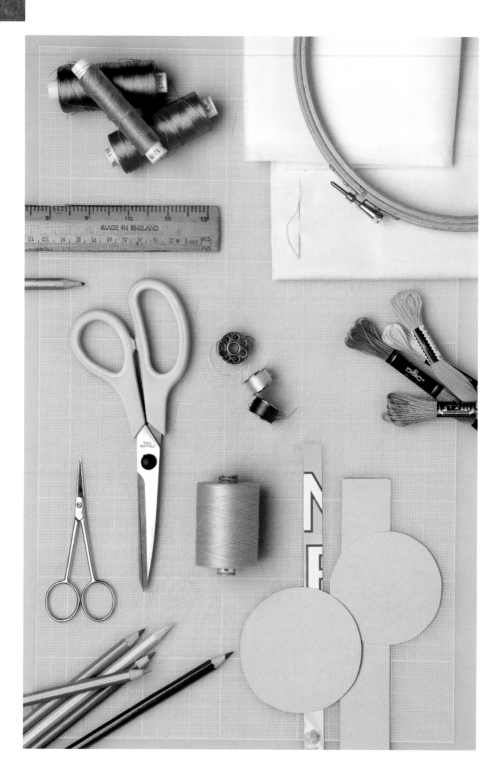

Tools and materials

A keepsake box

Make a lovely embroidered box either to keep your secrets of how to mix thread colours together, or to keep your new machine embroidery jewellery in – or both! The finished size of the box is 8 x 8 x 4 cm (3¼ x 3¼ x 1¾ in.).

YOU WILL NEED
Items from the 'basic tools' list plus:

- Thin card (an empty cereal box is ideal)
- A compass and pencil
- Heavyweight calico measuring 60 x 35 cm (23¾ x 13¾ in.)
- Stabilising fabric measuring 50 cm x 25 cm (19¾ x 10 in.)
- Embroidery or machine sewing threads in either 30 or 40 weights in:
  - black – outlines and decorative lines
  - turquoise – background
  - orange – daisy centre
  - yellow – daisy petals
  - lime green – decorative lines
  - cerise pink – daisy centre and daisy petal bobbin colour
- Five hand embroidery threads in orange, yellow, lime green, black and cerise pink
- Turquoise polyester sewing thread.

GETTING STARTED
You first need to make cardboard templates. There are four pieces to the box structure: the top lid, the lid lip, the base, and the base side. The top and top lip are slightly bigger than the base and base side to give a nice fit.

Using a ruler, pencil and compass, draw these four templates onto the card:
- The lid: a circle of 8 cm (3¼ in.) in diameter
- The base: a circle of 7 cm (2¾ in.) in diameter
- The lid lip: a rectangle of 28.5 x 1 cm (11¼ x ½ in.)
- The base side: a rectangle of 26.5 x 3 cm (10¼ x 1¼ in.)

These sizes are 'working sizes'. The stitch tension and how dense your stitches are will determine if you need to increase or decrease the sizes of the box component pieces – this is explained later in the project before you begin to edge and finish off the pieces.

Step 1

Cut out the four card shapes and draw round the top lid piece onto a piece of paper. Using a pencil, draw a daisy design (or one of your own) onto the paper shape and colour it using the coloured pencils to make a template for reference. On the calico, draw round all four card templates with the fabric drawing pen. Stick the paper drawing onto a light box or window pane, and stick the calico on top, lining up the paper box lid design with the box lid shape on the calico. Draw the design onto the calico box lid using fabric drawing pen.

Step 2

Fill a bobbin and thread the top of the machine with black thread in either a 30 or 40 weight and insert the calico into the embroidery hoop. Follow the design pattern on the box lid shape with the sewing machine needle and black thread. Go over the design twice to give a solid black stitch line to the daisy shape. When completed, take the embroidery hoop away from the machine and cut off the threads close to the embroidery.

Step 3

You are now going to mix the thread colours together to create little spots of the bobbin thread coming up into the top thread colour, as described in 'Mixing colours' on page 39. The colour combination of orange and cerise pink for the centre of the daisy will be quite subtle but the yellow and cerise pink for the petals will be a dramatic splash of colour.

Tighten the top sewing tension. Fill a bobbin with the cerise pink and thread the machine in orange thread. Try out this colour combination on the 'waste' base fabric surrounding the box lid and box bottom shapes. When you are satisfied with the colour mix of threads, fill in the daisy centre. Sew your lines of stitches in one direction so that the embroidery sits relatively flat; circles of stitches will cause the embroidery to become convex and difficult to work on. When the centre of the daisy has been embroidered, take the hoop away from the machine and cut off the top and bobbin threads. Change the top thread to yellow, keeping the cerise pink in the bobbin. Embroider the petals using the same tension and technique, this time taking the stitch lines from the inside edge nearest the middle of the daisy to the outside edge of the daisy petals.

Step 4

When all the petals have been embroidered, take the hoop away from the machine and cut off the top and bobbin threads. Change the top tension back to 'ordinary sewing' and thread the machine and fill a bobbin with turquoise

Colour in your templates

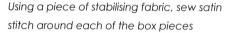

Using a piece of stabilising fabric, sew satin stitch around each of the box pieces

Twist the hand embroidery threads and sew a zigzag stitch over them

thread. To make sure the stitches are not too tight and that the bobbin thread is no longer being brought up onto the top surface, test the stitch on the 'waste' base fabric. When you are satisfied, embroider around the daisy petals, with the stitch lines going in one direction, until all the background has been filled in.

Step 5

Change the top thread to the lime green, keeping the turquoise thread in the bobbin. Starting on the very outside of the circle, run the stitch line towards the daisy petal and back again so you have a line measuring about 7 mm (½ in.). Take the stitch line onto the 'waste' fabric and run it alongside the edge of the box lid circle shape for about 7 mm (½ in.), and again run the stitch in, then out onto the waste base fabric. Repeat the process until you are back where you began. You now have a row of lime green lines. Change the top and bobbin threads to black, and between the lines of lime green sew a line measuring about 4 mm (¼ in.), and again take the stitch line out onto the waste base fabric. Run it alongside the circle edge for about 7 mm (½ in.), then take the line back into the box top piece and out. Repeat the same process until you reach where you began. You now have smaller lines of black in between the lines of lime green and the box lid is finished. Take the hoop out from under the machine and cut off the top and bobbin threads close to the embroidery.

Embroider all the template pieces

Step 6

Re-thread the machine with the turquoise thread and embroider the box bottom base, taking the stitch lines in one direction until all the base has been filled in. Still using the turquoise thread, embroider the top lip and base side, again taking the stitch line in one direction. Fill in as much of the box component shapes as possible before you move the embroidery hoop down and over the rest of the box top lip and base side.

Step 7

Change the top thread to the lime green and stitch over the base side to create vertical lines at intervals of 1.5 cm (¾ in.) all along this base side. Change the top and bobbin thread to black and sew a line between each of the lime green lines in the same manner. You thus produce a pattern of lime green and black stripes.

When this process is complete, cut off the top and bobbin threads and move the calico in the hoop to work on the rest of the box lid and base side. Continue to embroider with the turquoise thread first, then the lines of lime green, and finally the black, until all the component pieces have been solidly stitched in. Cut off the top and bobbin threads and any stray ends, and remove the calico from the hoop. Steam iron the backs of the four pieces to press and flatten them slightly, and to remove any whelp marks left by the hoop. (NB: First make sure that the hot iron will not melt any of the threads.)

Step 8

Cut around the box top and box base using sharp scissors, leaving a calico border of about 5 mm (¼ in.). Place the box top piece onto the stabilising fabric, making sure the fabric is bigger than the top of the box piece by 3 cm (1¼ in.) all the way round. Fit an ordinary sewing foot onto your sewing machine, thread the machine in the turquoise thread and raise the feed dog. Follow the instructions for the edging technique as described in 'Making a sample heart' (page 21) using hand embroidery thread colours for the twist in orange, yellow, lime green, black and cerise pink.

When the edging has been completed, sew the thread ends into the back of the satin stitch border and then place the box base piece onto another piece of stabilising fabric and repeat the same finishing-off process. These two box component pieces are the guide size to the top lip and base side pieces.

Step 9

Cut the calico off the top lip piece, leaving a border of 5 mm (¼ in.) all the way round and bend the lip around the outside of the lid piece. The lip will overrun itself so you will need to cut off one of the lip ends so it comfortably fits the outside edge of the box top shape. Once you are satisfied with the size, finish off the top lip piece by cutting and edging in the same way as the top and base of the box.

Step 10

Cut the last piece from the calico, i.e. the base side, again leaving a border of 5 mm (¼ in.) and bend this piece around the edge of the base bottom. One of the ends will need to be cut so that it meets correctly with no overlap, then edge and finish off this piece like the others.

Step 11

The four box component pieces are now ready to be hand sewn together, starting with the lid and the lid lip piece, then the base and the side. Thread the hand sewing needle with the polyester thread and run it through the beeswax, then tie the end of the thread with a small discreet knot. Using overstitch, sew through the twist on the edge of the piece to connect the two ends of the box lip band together to form a ring shape. Still using overstitch, sew the box top lip and the box top together to make the completed lid, making sure that when these two pieces have been sewn together you make a secure knot. Cut off the waste thread.

Sew the box side ends together in overstitch to form another ring shape. Then sew the box base piece and the box side piece together, again knotting the polyester thread and securely finishing off. Your box is now finished so you can fit the lid onto the base.

Hand sew the box component pieces together to form the box

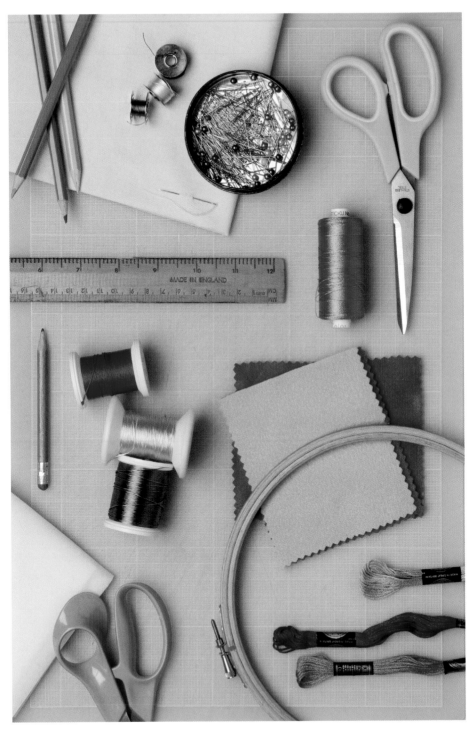

Tools and materials

A needle case

This practical and stylish needle case is made using thick and thin threads for a wonderful texture. The finished size of the folded case is 10 x 7.5 cm (4 x 3 in.).

YOU WILL NEED

Items from the 'basic tools' list plus:

- Heavyweight calico measuring 30.5 x 30.5 cm (12 x 12 in.)
- Stabilising fabric measuring 21 x 24 cm (8¼ x 9½ in.)
- Two pieces of felt in the colours of red and yellow, both measuring 10 x 12 cm (4 x 4¾ in.)
- Embroidery/ordinary sewing machine threads in 30 or 40 weights in:
  - black – outlines
  - mint green – main colour
  - lilac – design pattern shape
  - white – design pattern shape
  - red – design pattern shape
  - yellow – design pattern shape
- Thick thread in:
  - lilac – design pattern shape
  - white – design pattern shape
  - red – design pattern shape
  - yellow – design pattern shape
- Five hand embroidery threads in mint green, lilac, white, red and yellow
- A hand-sewing needle
- Pinking sheers
- Dressmaking pins

GETTING STARTED

Using an HB pencil and paper, draw the outline of a rectangle measuring 10 x 15 cm (4 x 6 in.) and a vertical line through its centre to indicate where the fold of the needle case will be. Draw a design of a semi-circle approx. 1.5cm (¾ in.) thick on each straight edge of the rectangle and, using coloured pencils, colour it in. At the top of the rectangle write the word 'top', and similarly indicate the right-hand side, left-hand side and bottom.

Using the masking tape, stick the paper design onto either a light box or window pane, and stick the piece of calico over the top. Using the fabric drawing pen,

trace the rectangle outline and the design onto the calico. Again draw a vertical line through the centre of the design to indicate where the fold will be, extending it by 1 cm (½ in.) beyond the outline of the box onto the waste base fabric, so that you still have reference to the fold line when the middle has been embroidered over.

Keep the drawing close at hand so you can refer to it while sewing as you will be working on the back of the calico to begin with, and need to know where the correct top, bottom, right and left sides of the design are as you embroider.

Step 1

Adjust your machine to embroidery/ darning mode and put the calico into the embroidery hoop. Thread the machine and wind a bobbin in black thread and carefully stitch along the drawn lines, which are your pattern guide for filling in.

Embroider your design working on the back of your piece

Step 2

Take the embroidery hoop away from the machine and cut off the top and bobbin threads close to the embroidery. Take the calico out of the hoop and turn the fabric over so that the back of the calico is facing upwards, then put the fabric back into the hoop.

Working on the back of your design, the next stage is to embroider with a combination of thick and thin threads. As the thick thread cannot be threaded through the machine, you have to embroider the work upside down and back to front. To complete this task see 'Thick thread' on page 41.

The thick thread will come out on the back; this will be the front when the needle case is finished

Step 3

Wind four bobbins, one of each in the thick thread colours of red, yellow, lilac and white. Put the bobbin of thick red thread into the bobbin case and thread the machine with the 30 or 40 weight yellow thread. Remember that you are working on the back of the piece and therefore the design is back to front, so refer to the paper template for the correct design format.

Bring up the bobbin thread on the calico at the same point as the red design shape is on the paper. The thick thread may be a little more difficult to bring up because of its bulk. Embroider this first shape. It may seem a little strange at first because you are working upside down and everything including the thread colours is in reverse. However, it is always exciting to see what the 'right' side looks like when all the sewing on the 'back' has been done.

Do not worry if small gaps in between the yellow stitches show some base fabric because, due to its thickness, the thread underneath is filling the area much quicker. Once you have embroidered all the yellow areas, take the hoop out of the machine and cut off the threads close to the embroidery.

Step 4

Change to the thick yellow thread bobbin and thread the machine in 30 or 40 weight red thread, and embroider the next piece of the design. Then change the bobbin and top threads and continue filling in the other two parts of the design using the thread combinations of thick white thread and 30 or 40 weight lilac and, lastly, thick lilac thread and 30 or 40 weight white. Refer to your paper design for the correct colouring.

Sew satin stitch to create a spine for the needle case

Use running stitch along the centre crease of the felt pieces, to create a 'spine'

Step 5

Take the calico out of the hoop, turn the fabric over and put it back in with the right side facing upwards. Using mint green thread in the 30 or 40 weight on both the top of the machine and in the bobbin, embroider the remaining areas of the design. Stitch in any direction you wish as this will add even more texture and form to the cover of your needle case.

Step 6

Take the hoop away from the sewing machine, cut off the top and bobbin threads near to the embroidery plus any other stray threads. As the case will be constantly opened and closed and both sides will be seen, it is important to have the back of the embroidery as neat as the front. Take the calico out of the hoop and steam iron the piece. (NB: First make sure that the hot iron will not melt any of the threads.)

Step 7

Fit an ordinary sewing foot onto the machine and, keeping the mint green thread, raise the dog feed. Set the zigzag dial to 'wide stitch' and the stitch length to 'close together' to create a satin stitch. Test this first on a waste piece of fabric, then sew the satin stitch along the fold line marked on the calico to create a spine for the needle case. Cut off the waste threads.

Step 8

Follow the instructions for the edging technique as described in 'Making a sample heart' (page 21) using hand embroidery thread colours for the twist in mint green, lilac, white, red and yellow. When the edging has been completed sew the thread ends into the back of the satin stitch border. Using a hot steam iron, press the piece in half along the satin stitch centre line to create the spine,

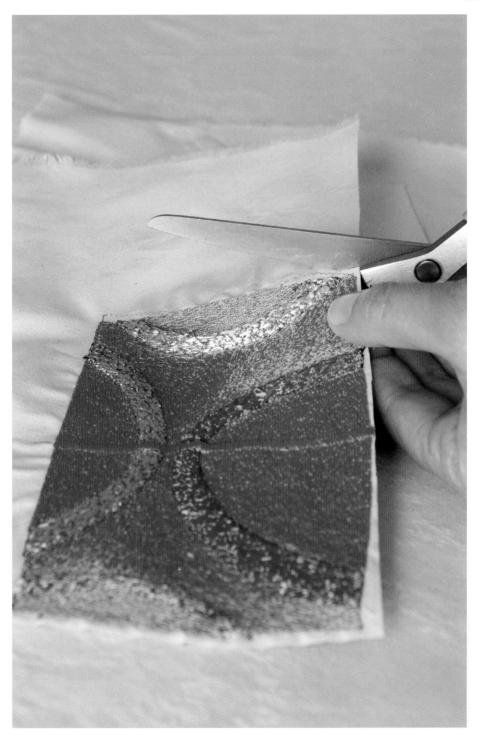

Cut the needle case from the calico

so that the case stays folded in half. If you have used threads which are likely to melt, fold the case in half along the spine and put the case either in a flower press or between heavy books for a couple of hours to encourage the crease.

Step 9

Using pinking sheers, cut the piece of red felt to 10 x 12 cm (4 x 4¾ in.) and the yellow piece to 9.5 x 11.5 cm (3¾ x 4½ in.). Fold the two pieces in half together with the red piece on the outside and measuring 10 x 6 cm (3¾ x 2½ in.). Mark the crease with a dressmaking pin at the top and bottom of the crease. Set the machine tension to 'ordinary sewing' mode and sew a line along the crease, leaving long sewing threads at the beginning and at the end of the stitch line. Take out the pins then cut off the threads, leaving long lengths.

Thread the top two long threads into a hand sewing needle and sew the felt pieces into the spine of the embroidered piece and, similarly, sew the two long threads from the bottom of the felt pieces into the spine and secure with discreet knots.

The needle case is now finished and ready to be filled with needles and pins!

Sew the felt pieces into the needle case

A photo frame

Brighten up a plain wooden frame with your very own embroidered frame surround. The finished size of the embroidered frame is 19 x 14.5 cm (7½ x 5¾ in.).

YOU WILL NEED

Items from the 'basic tools' list plus:

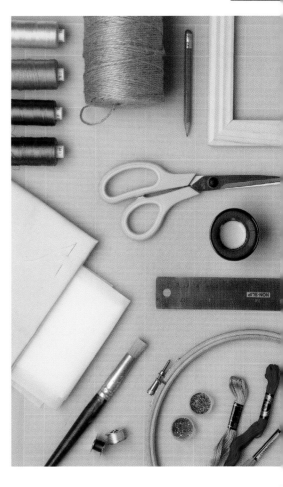

Tools and materials for the embroidered frame

- A wooden picture frame with a flat wooden surround approximately 2.5 cm (1 in.) wide
- Heavyweight calico measuring 30.5 x 30.5 cm (12 x 12 in.)
- Stabilising fabric measuring 26 x 23 cm (10¼ x 9 in.)
- Embroidery/ordinary sewing machine threads in 30 or 40 weights in:
    - black – outlines
    - yellow – flower centre
    - orange – flower outer centre
    - cerise pink – flower petals
    - moss green – leaves
    - sage green – leaves
    - forest green – leaves
    - dark green – leaf spines
    - pale blue – background
- Five hand embroidery threads in the colours of cerise pink, moss green, forest green, orange and yellow
- A hand-sewing needle
- A beading needle
- Red polyester thread
- Tiny red glass beads
- Beeswax
- An adhesive glue suitable for wood and textiles

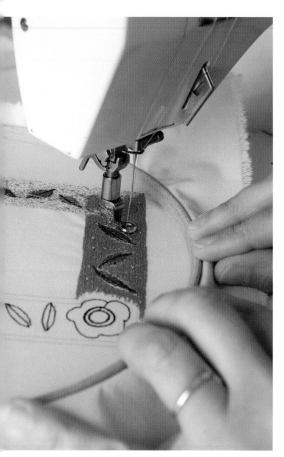

GETTING STARTED

Dismantle the wooden picture frame, keeping all the components safe as you will need these when you reassemble it later. Using an HB pencil and paper, draw round the outside and inside of the empty frame. Then measure with a ruler to increase the size of the frame template on both the outside and inside edges by 5 mm (¼ in.). For the design, draw a flower in each corner and leaves regularly spaced around the frame, and colour these in using coloured pencils.

Stick the paper drawing onto a light box or window pane with masking tape and stick the calico over the top. Trace the design and the frame template onto the calico using the fabric drawing pen. Then position the design near to where you are sitting so you can easily see it while sewing.

Embroider the flowers, leaves and then the background

Step 1

Thread the machine and wind a bobbin in black thread. Put the calico in the embroidery hoop and embroider the outlines of the design. Re-thread the machine and wind a bobbin in yellow thread and embroider the centre of the flowers in either a horizontal or vertical direction rather than a circular motion to avoid the embroidery from becoming convex. Continue to embroider the rest of the flowers using first the orange thread and then the cerise pink thread, using the same colour on the top and in the bobbin.

Step 2

Embroider the leaves in the three shades of green, taking the stitch direction from the bottom of each individual leaf to its tip. Change the thread colour on both the top and in the bobbin to pale blue and embroider the background in a clockwise direction around the frame, so that all the stitch lines run parallel with the frame surround. Change to dark green thread and run a stitch line up the middle of each leaf to denote the skeleton structure of the leaves.

Step 3

Garnish the pale blue surface with zigzag spots of cerise pink, yellow and orange. See 'Mixing colours' on page 39 for how to create this effect. Test the technique on the 'waste' base fabric in the middle of the frame piece, and when you are happy with the size of the spots, embroider them onto the actual piece.

Step 4

Take the piece out of the hoop and with a hot steam iron press the piece flat. (NB: First make sure that the hot iron will not melt any of the threads.) Cut the embroidery piece from the calico leaving a border of 5 mm (¼ in.) on both the inside and the outside of the frame.

Step 5

Fit an ordinary sewing foot and keep the pale blue thread on your machine.

Sew satin stitch on the inside and outside edges

Place the piece onto some stabilising fabric and follow the instructions for the edging technique described in 'Making a sample heart' on page 21. First edge the inside border of the frame and then the outside. The hand embroidery thread colours to be used in the twist are cerise pink, moss green, forest green, orange and yellow. When both the edges have been completed sew the thread ends into the back of the satin stitch borders.

Step 6

Thread the beading needle with the red polyester thread and run it through beeswax. Sew five glass beads individually into the centre of each of the four flower motifs in the four corners of the embroidered frame. Knot and secure the thread and cut off any stray threads from the back of the piece.

Sew the tiny glass beads into the middle of
the flower motif by hand

Step 7

Using adhesive, stick the machine embroidery piece to the wooden frame.
(NB: Test the glue on a waste piece of embroidery before using it on the
finished piece to make sure the glue will not seep through the embroidery.)
When the glue is dry, reassemble the frame and insert a photograph or picture
of your choice.

Glue the embroidered frame onto the wooden picture frame

Bloomin' Rain *by Linda Miller 2007 16 x 13 cm (6¼ x 5 in.)*

Silkie Soft *by Linda Miller 2008 16 x 44 cm (6½ x 17½ in.)*

Glossary

Base fabric The calico or other fabric which is being machine embroidered onto.

Beeswax Running a piece of beeswax across hand sewing thread coats and prevents it from becoming knotted and tangled, thus enabling the thread, when sewing, to pass through the fabric easily.

Calico A cream-coloured plain weave 100% cotton fabric.

Cutting mat A self-healing mat with a measuring grid imprint. Paper and fabric can be cut on it using a craft knife without damaging the mat surface.

D-rings Used in pairs and shaped like the letter 'D', when these metal rings are screwed into the back of a wooden picture frame they support the cord which enables the frame to be hung.

Daylight simulation bulbs A light-bulb that has been manufactured to give a 'daylight' light to improve clarity and contrast.

Dissolvable fabric/water-soluble fabric A translucent water-soluble fabric which when washed in warm water disappears to leave only the embroidery stitches behind.

Embroidery/darning foot A sewing machine foot designed for either machine embroidery or darning damaged fabric.

Epoxy resin adhesive An adhesive and hardener which when mixed together in equal parts form a strong bonding adhesive.

Fabric pen A permanent fabric marker pen which will not bleed into the fabric or embroidery.

Feed dog Situated in the base plate of a sewing machine where the needle goes in and out, the feed dog teeth can be lowered and raised by a switch, or may have a plate fitted over them (refer to the sewing machine manual).

Iron-on Vilene A fusible interfacing to add firmness to fabrics. The shiny (adhesive) side is bonded onto the fabric by the heat from an iron.

Light box A wooden or metal box with translucent perspex on the top and a light inside.

Masking tape A paper tape which is easy to tear and can be drawn on. It can be used temporarily to stick fabric and paper together and to cover fabric edges to stop them from fraying. It is also used in the decorating trade to mask areas, such as glass panels in doors, etc.

Sewing machine needle numbers The Imperial (USA) numbers are the smaller numbers and the metric (European) numbers are the higher numbers, e.g. 9/65 11/75 12/80 14/90 16/100 18/110.

Stabilising fabric Placed beneath delicate fabrics such as silk and fine cottons, the stabilising fabric is used to prevent tearing and wrinkling during stitching. It is a fine, interfacing style fabric which can be easily torn or cut away once all the desired stitching has been completed.

Thread weights The weight of a thread is based on its length and not on its heaviness. Its title is derived from how many kilometres it takes to equal one kilogram, e.g. 40 kilometres of a 40 weight thread weighs 1 kilogram. The lower the number of the thread, the thicker it is, e.g. 30 weight thread is thicker than a 40 weight thread.

Translucent sticky tape A translucent sticky tape which can be drawn on and sticks paper and fabric together temporarily.

Waste base fabric The unstitched fabric surrounding the machine embroidery.

Directory

Suppliers – UK

Embroidery threads and sundry items
Cotton Patch
1283–1285 Stratford Road
Hall Green
Birmingham B28 9AJ
Tel: +44 (0) 121 702 2840
mailorder@cottonpatch.co.uk
www.cottonpatch.co.uk

Fabric suppliers
Whaleys (Bradford) Ltd
Harris Court
Great Horton
Bradford BD7 4EQ
Tel: +44 (0) 1274 576718
Fax: +44 (0) 1274 521309
info@whaleysltd.co.uk
www.whaleys-bradford.ltd.uk

Fabric suppliers, threads, sewing sundries
John Lewis
171 Victoria Street
London SW1E 5NN
Tel: +44 (0) 20 7828 1000
www.johnlewis.com

Barnyarns (Ripon) Ltd
Canal Wharf
Bongate Green
Ripon
North Yorkshire HG4 1AQ
Tel: +44 (0) 1765 690069
www.barnyarns.co.uk

Texere Yarns
College Mill
Barkerend Road
Bradford BD1 4AU
Tel: +44 (0) 1274 722191
info@texereyarns.co.uk
www.texere.co.uk

Silken Strands
20 Y Rhos
Bangor
Gwynedd LL57 2LT
Wales
Tel: +44 (0) 1248 362 361
sales@silkenstrands.co.uk
www.silkenstrands.co.uk

Coats Crafts UK
PO Box 22
Lingfield House
Lingfield Point
McMullen Road
Darlington
County Durham DL1 1YJ
Tel: +44 (0) 1325 394237
enquiries.ccuk@coats.com
www.coatscrafts.co.uk

Craft sundries and frames
Hobby Craft
www.hobbycraft.co.uk

Frames and suppliers
Zanart Gallery and Framing T/A The Picture Framing Experts
13 Dane Lane
Wilstead
Bedford MK45 3HT
Tel: 0870 9747058
www.thepictureframingexperts.co.uk

Wessex Picture Frames

Gordleton Industrial Park

Hannah Way

Sway Road

Pennington

Lymington

Hants SO41 8JD

Tel: +44 (0) 1590 681681

www.wessexpictures.com

Sewing machines

Bogod & Co Ltd

Tel: +44 (0) 20 7549 7849

sales@bernina.co.uk

www.berninaukshop.co.uk

Direct Sewing Machines

266 Battersea Park Road

London SW11 3BP

Tel: +44 (0) 207 738 9040

enquires@directsewingmachines.co.uk

www.directsewingmachines.co.uk

Suppliers – USA

Maderia Threads USA

AllStitch Embroidery Supplies

3031 James St.

Baltimore

MD 21230–1035

Tel: 410-646-0382

CustomerService@AllStitch.net

Index